Managing Your Company Cars

In Nine Easy Steps

Colin Tourick

in association with
Daimler Fleet Management

Managing Your Company Cars In Nine Easy Steps

© Colin Tourick 2008
in association with Daimler Fleet Management

First published in Great Britain by Eyelevel Books, 2008

www.eyelevelbooks.co.uk

Printed in Great Britain by Biddles Limited, King's Lynn

ISBN 978 1902528 243

Running a car fleet is hard work. There is an awful lot to learn and traditionally much of this knowledge has been picked up on the job. For a long time I felt there was a need for a textbook for fleet managers so when I wrote *Managing Your Company Cars* I was pleased it was so well received. It seemed fleet managers agreed with me. Strong demand for the first edition encouraged me to write the second edition.

However, fleet managers are busy people and at 520 pages *Managing Your Company Cars* takes quite a time to read. That's the reason for producing this new book, *Managing Your Company Cars in Nine Easy Steps*. It takes the core material from *Managing Your Company Cars* and distils it into a much slimmer volume.

To prolong this book's shelf life I have deliberately ignored topics that might be hitting the fleet headlines at present but which are less likely to be of pressing interest in a few years or which will no longer be relevant or accurate.

So, for example, tax incentives to encourage biofuels are omitted. Indeed, most taxes change frequently so they are largely omitted except where this might leave the reader confused. For example, a discussion of employee car ownership schemes cannot get very far without mentioning income tax, national insurance and approved mileage allowance rates.

As *Managing Your Company Cars* has sold in 26 countries across 6 continents this new book omits some issues that would only be of interest to UK-based readers.

To help the reader and hopefully make this book easier to read, I tend to refer to 'you' rather than 'the fleet manager', 'the borrower', 'the lessee', 'your company', 'your business' or 'the client'.

A hearty thank you to Paul Harrop, sales and marketing director of Daimler Fleet Management, Rachel Mills of Colin Tourick & Associates Limited and Vera Tourick, for reading the proofs.

Finally, I welcome feedback. You can reach me via www.tourick.com

Professor Colin Tourick MSc FCA FCCA MICFM is a management consultant specialising in fleet management.

Colin's fleet career started in 1980 when he was the first accountant at LeasePlan UK. He then spent five years in big ticket leasing in the City of London financing aircraft, ships and property. He was general manager of Fleet Motor Management, director of Commercial Union Vehicle Finance and corporate finance director of BNP Paribas' leasing subsidiary. For six years he was managing director of CitiCapital Fleet.

He currently works for some of the largest banks, motor manufacturers and vehicle leasing companies, in the UK and abroad.

Colin has served as chairman of the British Vehicle Rental and Leasing Association Training Committee, a member of the BVRLA Leasing and Fleet Management Committee and a member of the Finance & Leasing Association's Motor Finance Committee. He is a chartered accountant, a certified accountant and a member of the Institute of Car Fleet Management. He has a Master of Science degree in Accounting and Finance from London School of Economics and is a Visiting Professor of the Centre for Automotive Management at the University of Buckingham Business School.

He is a frequent commentator, writer and speaker on fleet industry issues. His particular interests are reducing fleet management costs and building successful vehicle management businesses.

Further information is available from www.tourick.com.

Also by the author:
Managing Your Company Cars
Published by Eyelevel Books in association with Daimler Fleet Management
ISBN 1 902528 21 2
See page 117 for details

CONTENTS

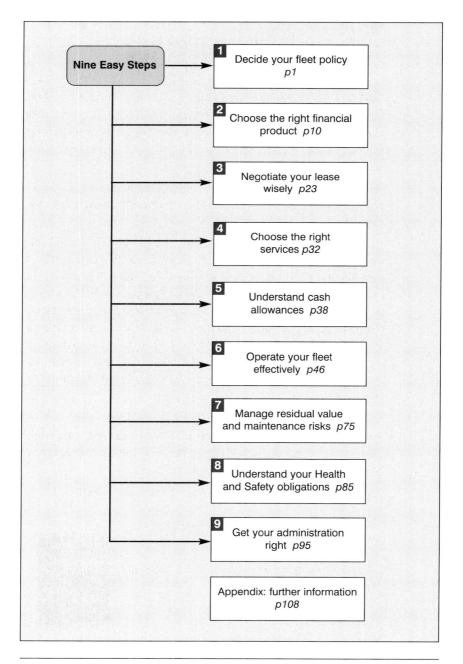

1 DECIDE YOUR FLEET POLICY

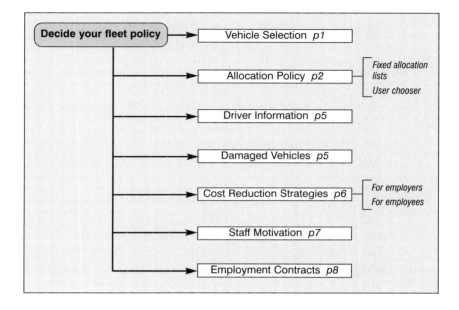

'Fleet policy' is a fleet industry expression. It means all of your organisation's policies and procedures for running its car fleet, including the vehicles you select, whether you allow your drivers to choose their vehicles, whether they are allowed to contribute extra ('trade up') to get a better car, your policies for dealing with driver safety, what happens if a driver returns a vehicle in poor condition and so on. Your fleet policy should be set out in writing and this document – the **Company Car Policy** – should be handed to each driver.

VEHICLE SELECTION

Every vehicle your company uses should be fit for the tasks it will be required to do.

If it is to be used by a sales engineer to carry heavy loads, the maximum load weight, carrying capacity and sill height will be important. If the sales manager will regularly use it for long-distance motorway driving, a larger engine and longer wheelbase will make his journey more comfortable and therefore safer.

Some city centres will soon ban high-emission vehicles. If your drivers routinely drive in these cities they should be allocated low-emission vehicles.

Fleet managers have learned the hard way not to give high performance cars to young, inexperienced drivers as this can lead to expensive mistakes or worse.

You will need to consider the type of fuel, number of doors and whether the vehicle transmission needs to be manual or automatic.

If you allow your employees to select optional extras, be aware that some extras enhance resale values while others do not. For example, leather seating will enhance value in high-value cars but not in basic models. Alloy wheels can cost more to buy and to run; if they are in good condition they enhance resale value but if damaged they can reduce it by hundreds of pounds.

The vehicles you select should reflect your company's image and the industry in which you operate. If you sell luxury goods to the landed gentry, arriving in a small basic car may not project the right image. And if your company's image is 'green', your fleet should reflect this.

ALLOCATION POLICY

Having considered the most appropriate vehicles for the job, you need to set an allocation policy – deciding who gets what. Most organisations allocate vehicles according to staff grade but many now allow their employees to choose vehicles that meet private as well as business needs. So, if an engineer has young children she may prefer to have an estate car instead of a van.

Such flexibility is good for staff motivation and morale but if you offer too much flexibility the costs can begin to rise.

A good approach to vehicle allocation is to select a benchmark car for each group of drivers (sales representatives, middle management, directors, etc) and build your list from there, using whole-life costs (see below) rather than list price.

You must allocate cars without discriminating between men and women. In 2003 a group of women won a discrimination case at an Industrial Tribunal because their male colleagues were allowed better cars under their company's car scheme.

Some companies allow employees to contribute to the cost of a more expensive vehicle ('trade up') and to pay either by monthly deduction from salary or a lump sum on delivery of the vehicle. Some also allow employees to trade down and take some extra salary, which can be useful for a perk car driver if their partner already has a car.

If used cars are allocated, the policy should specify how long they will be kept.

Your vehicle allocation policy will need to be updated when vehicle models are discontinued, new cars are released and when list prices change.

FIXED ALLOCATION LISTS

You can publish a fixed list that sets out all of the vehicles available for each grade of driver or you can allow drivers to choose their own cars.

A fixed list gives you certainty and control. Fewer anomalies will arise and your staff will easily understand the system.

However, if you change the list infrequently the business will bear the increased cost when car prices rise. You will not be able to remove them from the list until the next review date. On the other hand, if you change the list frequently a vehicle available to a group of drivers one day will be unavailable to them the next day, if a price rise has put the car out of their range.

A fixed list containing only high-emission vehicles will be a cause of employee dissatisfaction. You will be forcing your drivers to pay high levels of personal tax on their vehicles.

Fixed lists tend to be poor for employee morale.

USER CHOOSER

This is the alternative to the fixed list. The driver chooses a vehicle based on their seniority and the cost of the vehicle.

This can cause problems when the driver leaves and the company finds the car is not suitable to allocate to any other employee. This problem does not arise with a fixed list.

Some companies allow their drivers to select vehicles based on the manufacturers' published list prices. However, this approach is sub-optimal because list prices ignore the different discounts available on different vehicles.

Alternatively you might allow drivers to choose any car up to a limit based on the cost to the business net of discounts. This is better than selection based on list price. However, invoice price does not reflect the full cost of the vehicle to your business over the period in which you will use it.

Allowing drivers to select cars up to the value of the contract hire rental of a particular benchmark car represents a further improvement, because the rental automatically reflects purchase discounts, depreciation and interest costs. However, the contract hire rental does not include fuel costs (which may be relevant where the employer reimburses actual fuel cost rather than paying a flat amount per business mile) or insurance premiums.

Whole-life cost reflects the total cost of using the car over the period in which it will be retained by the business. It includes depreciation, interest, servicing, maintenance and repairs. Fuel costs can be added if the company pays for fuel. Whole-life cost represents the best form of allocation policy.

Whole-life costs will increase if a driver chooses a vehicle specification that will be unattractive to buyers when the time comes to sell the vehicle. For example: Air-conditioning is essential on large cars and is becoming important on medium-size cars. Electric windows are essential on prestige cars. Alloy wheels are essential on sporty cars. Metallic paint looks better on most cars (but not vans). Without these, the resale value of a vehicle will be much reduced and the whole-life cost will rise.

You can obtain whole-life cost data from magazines, fleet

management and contract hire companies, motoring organisations and specialist publishers.

DRIVER INFORMATION

It is good practice to place a **driver handbook** or instruction card in each car. This can be a condensed version of the instructions set out in the Company Car Policy.

It should say what to do in the event of an accident or breakdown, where to get the vehicle serviced, where to obtain tyres, brakes, exhausts and replacement windscreens, what to do if a new tax disc or MoT certificate has not arrived by the due date and what to do if a rental car is required.

DAMAGED VEHICLES

A driver has returned his vehicle and you are not happy with the condition. What should you do about it? Should you charge him for the damage and, if so, how much?

It may help you to know that 25% of companies do nothing if the driver returns a car in an unacceptable condition, 40% recharge the cost of restitution to the driver, 40% charge the cost centre and 30% take disciplinary action against the driver. (These total more than 100% because some companies take more than one of these actions.)

The **BVRLA Fair Wear and Tear Guide** discusses the dividing line between acceptable wear and tear and unacceptable damage. If a leased vehicle is returned in unacceptable condition the leasing company will probably invoice you for the damage. If you plan to charge the employee for damage, you might choose to charge them this amount. However, if the car is not leased no one will send you an invoice for the cost of the damage; you will just receive less when the car is sold and will have to find some other way to work out how much to charge the employee.

As with all matters relating to fleet vehicles, if you have a clear company policy on vehicle damage at the outset and everyone knows what this is, you will have fewer problems later.

A reasonable policy might be to:

- Advise your drivers they have to look after their company vehicles and that they will be penalised for keeping them in an unsatisfactory condition.
- Issue them with a copy of the BVRLA Fair Wear and Tear Guide (www.bvrla.co.uk) or a similar document produced in-house.
- Say they will be recharged the cost the company incurs as a result of the unreasonable condition of the car, regardless of whether this arises through a recharge from a leasing company or a reduction in sale proceeds.
- Make it clear that failure to maintain the vehicle properly may lead to disciplinary action being taken, the withdrawal of the vehicle without compensation or its replacement with a smaller or cheaper model.
- Say that repeated damage may lead to disciplinary proceedings including, in an extreme case, dismissal for damaging company property.
- Instruct drivers to report all damage to you as soon as it occurs.
- Advise them that if they damage a vehicle they may have to undergo a course of driver training before being allowed to drive a company vehicle again.

Your policy should fit in with your fleet objectives and company culture.

COST-REDUCTION STRATEGIES

If cost reduction is very important to you, your fleet policy should reflect this. There are many ways to reduce your fleet costs.

FOR EMPLOYERS

- Don't provide free fuel for private mileage.
- Choose the right financial product for your fleet.

- Remember it's normally cheaper after tax to use a purchase-based finance product for expensive cars and a lease-based finance product for cheaper cars (see below).
- Move to a fixed list not a user chooser policy.
- Use whole-life costs to select vehicles for your fleet list.
- Remember that the weight of a car rather than its engine size determines fuel consumption.
- Make sure cars are serviced regularly to maintain fuel efficiency and to identify vehicle problems before they become expensive.
- Consider hiring cars rather than paying employees a mileage allowance to use their own cars.
- Consider having pool cars available for occasional journeys.
- Negotiate the best possible early termination clause in your contract hire agreement and avoid early termination charges by redeploying leased vehicles within the business.
- Renegotiate contract hire agreements mid-term rather than building up big excess mileage charges.
- If you have a large fleet, consider self-insuring the comprehensive risk.
- Consider introducing a cash-for-car or ECO scheme.
- Use journey-planning tools (see below).

For employees
- Consider taking a cash option if it is offered.
- Choose a low CO_2 vehicle, perhaps a diesel.
- Consider giving up free private fuel.

Staff motivation

Research has consistently shown that company cars are a most valued and prized employment benefit amongst UK employees, second only to pension benefits.

Our love affair with company cars is deeply entrenched and has survived the efforts of many governments to tax us out of them.

Many employees have chosen between two prospective employers on the basis of the quality and status of company car on offer.

You can demotivate staff by trying to remove cars or watering down the status of the cars on offer.

There is good evidence that staff enjoy having the flexibility to choose their own company car. Many companies offer 'cafeteria-style' flexible benefits systems that allow employees to choose their own benefits from a range of options. Employees like having the flexibility to contribute towards the cost of a more expensive car or to trade down to a smaller car and pocket the savings.

Around 50% of UK companies give their employees the option to take extra salary instead of a company car. This is called '**cash-for-car**' (see below and page 38). In most voluntary schemes the take-up of the cash option has been low and if employees are forced to give up company cars and asked to use their own cars for business, this can cause resentment.

EMPLOYMENT CONTRACTS

Employment contracts govern the relationship between employers and employees. The contract becomes relevant when you decide to change your company car policy, for example, by moving away from company cars to cash allowances; the contract may not allow you to do this unilaterally.

If you try to force people into a cash-for-car or ECO scheme when they have a contractual entitlement to a company car, you will be breaching their contracts of employment.

If an employee has been continuously employed for more than a year they can sue for breach of contract and unfair dismissal. Several groups of employees have engaged solicitors to act for them against their employers on precisely this issue – it's not a great way to motivate staff.

Without a contractual right to vary the employment contract you need the employees' consent to allow a cash-for-car scheme to be introduced.

Even if the employer does have the right to vary the contract this right should be exercised reasonably. 'Reasonably' here means that it should be reasonable from the employee's rather than the employer's perspective.

If you have a contractual right to alter the employment contract and decide to introduce a cash-for-car scheme that is fair and reasonable, the employee must go along with it or they can face the possibility of disciplinary action. If they refuse a reasonable request to change their employment contract they can be dismissed and offered re-employment on revised terms.

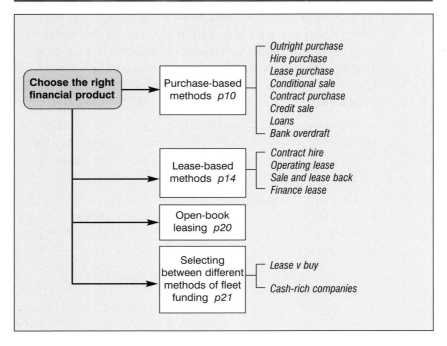

You can either purchase your cars or lease them.

PURCHASE-BASED METHODS

OUTRIGHT PURCHASE

This is the fleet industry's expression for when a business buys cars rather than using some form of finance or lease.

If you buy a vehicle you have to show it as an asset ('capitalise it') on your balance sheet. This may be undesirable for quoted companies as it adversely affects their return on asset ratios.

If you buy your vehicles you have to shop around to find them and negotiate the deals. Many companies find this to be an administrative headache.

If you like the idea of owning your vehicles, don't mind putting then on your balance sheet, like to be flexible about when you sell them and don't mind tying up working capital, outright purchase might be right for you. However, you will be fully exposed to movements in the used vehicle market when you come to sell them; ie you take the residual value risk. And you will not get the same levels of dealer and manufacturer discounts – 'volume related bonuses' – that leasing companies can attract.

HIRE PURCHASE

Hire purchase (HP) is *'a contract for the hire of an asset that contains a provision giving the hirer an option to acquire legal title to the asset upon the fulfilment of certain conditions stated in the contract'*.

The contract is a hire agreement and you will become the owner if you opt to acquire legal title (ownership) at the end of the agreement. For most people, HP is simply a method of buying a vehicle on deferred payment terms. Hence the client is normally called a 'buyer' rather than 'hirer' and the payments are called 'instalments' or 'payments' rather than 'rentals'.

The agreement will give you the option to buy the vehicle for a nominal 'bargain' amount. Unlike conditional sale, the right to buy is an option and not a contractual obligation. Normally, you will pay the option amount and take title.

Typically, the hire purchase payment pattern ('profile') will be 1 payment followed by 35 or 47 equal monthly payments starting one month after commencement of the agreement. A deposit may also be required.

A hire purchase agreement gives you all the risks and rewards of ownership from the date of delivery, including residual value risk. Therefore, the vehicle has to be shown as an asset on your balance sheet together with a corresponding liability representing the balance due to the funder, as if you financed it using a loan.

LEASE PURCHASE

This is the same as a hire purchase agreement but with a lump sum ('balloon') instalment payable at the end of the contract. If the balloon has been estimated accurately, the sale proceeds will cover the balloon payment so you will not be left out of pocket at the end of the contract.

CONDITIONAL SALE

Conditional sale is a finance agreement that contractually commits you to become the owner of the vehicle once all the payments have been made and conditions met.

It is non-cancellable and no 'option-to-purchase' fee is payable because title passes automatically when the last payment is made.

CONTRACT PURCHASE

This product combines three agreements; a lease purchase or conditional sale agreement containing a balloon payment, a repurchase undertaking and a maintenance agreement. The client agrees to buy the vehicle by paying instalments for a period of time and the supplier undertakes to buy it back at the end of the contract for a pre-agreed fixed price, at the client's option. Contract purchase is used by companies and consumers ('**personal contract purchase**' or '**PCP**').

As the underlying legal contract is a conditional sale or hire purchase agreement, under which you are buying the vehicle and assuming all the 'risks and rewards of ownership', contract purchase is always 'on balance sheet' if the customer is a business.

The repurchase price offered by the supplier represents their estimate of the likely future value of the vehicle. This pre-agreed price is usually called the guaranteed repurchase price, the guaranteed minimum purchase value or the **guaranteed minimum future value (GMFV)**. The supplier is at risk; they don't know if you will sell the vehicle back to them and they don't know what the market value of the vehicle will be should you decide to do so.

Contract purchase represents less than 5% of the fleet finance market and is a niche product. However, as PCP, it represents the majority of point-of-sale consumer finance deals arranged by car dealers.

CREDIT SALE

This is similar to hire purchase or conditional sale except that title to the vehicle passes to you at the start of the agreement rather than the end. Credit sale used to be uncommon because it requires the funder to give up the security of ownership of the asset. However we have seen more credit sale deals recently because of the growth in popularity of ECO schemes. Benefit in kind tax does not apply if title in the vehicle transfers to the employee, so ECO schemes use credit sale agreements to transfer ownership to the employee when the new vehicle is delivered.

LOANS

Many companies use loans to finance their vehicles. These loans are usually unsecured so the lender cannot repossess and sell the vehicle if the borrower stops paying. So unless your business is financially strong the interest rates will be high to compensate for the lender's lack of tangible security.

Loans can be obtained at fixed or variable interest rates and for short or long periods. They are simple to administer and do not require you to get involved in the complexities of lease accounting. Variable rate loans can often be repaid without penalty. Loan interest is normally deductible as a business expense for tax purposes. If you have title to a vehicle you can claim capital allowances (tax depreciation allowances). Vehicles financed on loans have to be disclosed ('capitalised') on your balance sheet.

BANK OVERDRAFT

The bank overdraft is the most widely used form of business finance in the UK. Most companies, even cash-rich ones, have an overdraft facility.

There is a limit to the size of overdraft facility your company will be able to obtain from its bank. That is because overdrafts are a type of working capital, designed to finance the trade cycle – the gap between buying goods and services to make your product and the day you are paid by your customer. If you use your overdraft to finance long term assets, such as vehicles, you may drain your company of its working capital.

Most overdrafts are offered as variable rate products. If you finance a vehicle for three years at fixed rates you will fix your outgoings over that period. Finance them on overdraft for three years and you will be exposed to interest rate changes during that time, so if rates rise you could end up paying much more than you had planned.

LEASE-BASED METHODS

CONTRACT HIRE

This is the most popular UK fleet funding product. Outside the UK it is called an operating lease or a closed-end lease.

Under contract hire, the supplier leases a vehicle to you for a fixed period and mileage, in return for a fixed rental. At the end of the lease, so long as the vehicle has not exceeded the agreed mileage and is in fair condition, you simply return it without further cost.

The supplier takes the residual value or 'RV' risk. If the vehicle sells for more or less than they estimated, they will make a profit or loss respectively.

Contract hire is offered '**maintenance-inclusive**' or '**without maintenance**'. If it includes maintenance, the supplier will pay for all standard servicing and maintenance work, vehicle excise duty, an agreed number of replacement tyres and membership of a roadside recovery service.

Motor insurance is usually excluded although other insurances are sometimes offered, eg credit payment insurance, mechanical breakdown insurance, early termination protection and gap insurance.

The agreement does not cover the cost of damage, neglect or wilful mistreatment, eg 'kerbed' tyres and wheels, engines being allowed to run dry, diesel fuel being pumped into petrol-engined cars, dented doors, broken mirrors or deep scratches. If the supplier pays for these you will be recharged.

If the supplier's estimate of the cost of maintaining the vehicle is too low, it will make a loss; if too high, it will make a profit. Therefore the supplier takes the 'maintenance risk' in the vehicle.

Most contract hire companies will only lease you a vehicle for between twelve months and five years, with three and four years being the most popular periods.

Contract hire rentals are fixed; they do not vary with changes in market interest rates, so you will not be taking any interest rate risk.

The quotation and agreement will show the maximum mileage allowed during the lease period. If this is exceeded, you will be charged an **excess mileage charge** to allow the supplier to recover the additional depreciation and maintenance costs.

If you lease several vehicles from one supplier, the agreement will normally include a '**pooled mileage**' clause to allow under-mileage driven by one car to be credited against over-mileage in another.

Some contract hire companies refuse to lease some vehicles, eg kit cars or extremely expensive cars, where it is difficult to set residual values and maintenance budgets as there are so few examples on the road.

The contract hire quote you receive will show the CO_2 output of the vehicle so that the driver can calculate the amount of benefit-in-kind tax payable.

All contract hire companies will allow you to terminate your lease early. They will charge you an amount to clear their books and any extra costs they may have to bear in keeping their own funding in place until the end of the lease. They may also charge for disrupting their capital allowance flows and for some of the profit they had hoped to make had the contract run to maturity.

Many contract hire agreements are silent on what happens on early termination but it is best to agree this in writing with the contract hire company up front.

There are several methods of calculating a contract hire early termination settlement figure. Under the **fixed number of rentals method**, you will pay perhaps 6 rentals if you terminate in the first

12 months, 4 in the next 12 months and 3 thereafter. Under the **actual cost method** the supplier simply charges the amount required to clear its books. This is sometimes seen in 'open-book' contract hire arrangements. Each company has its own approach.

In some cases a formula based on the number of rentals payable in future can give you a lower early termination charge than the actual cost method. Whatever early termination method is used, the amount payable will always include any arrears, interest on arrears, costs, fees or expenses that the supplier incurs in recovering and selling the vehicle.

If the agreement is regulated by the Consumer Credit Act, you have the right to hand the vehicle back after half the payments have been made.

If you know you are likely to need a vehicle for a short period, eg for an overseas visitor who is in the UK for a fixed period, or for someone who plans to retire in 18 months, you will save money by leasing for the shorter period rather than early terminating. If a driver leaves your employment it is usually cheaper to redeploy their leased vehicle within your business rather than handing it back and paying an early settlement charge. If you expect to have a high incidence of early termination, perhaps because you are in an industry with high staff turnover, consider taking ex-lease or used cars for some staff, to avoid early termination costs.

Normally, leasing companies are happy to extend a lease so long as you are not in default of your agreement. If you want to keep a vehicle for a short while longer they will normally allow you to do so at the same rental, without formality. If you want to extend it for, say, 6 months or more, they may agree to a formal extension and an agreement will be drawn up showing a new end date and a new rental.

Most contract hire agreements don't allow you to attach an accessory to the vehicle, or if they do they say it must be removed at your expense at the end of the lease without damaging the vehicle. If you want to add an accessory after delivery, speak to the contract hire company first.

At the end of the lease the contract hire company will contact you to arrange vehicle collection. The collection agent will complete a report for both parties to sign, confirming the vehicle has been handed over and noting any damage. Many contract hire companies will deliver a driver's new vehicle and collect his ex-lease vehicle at the same time. This is '**key-for-key exchange**' and it has obvious advantages for everyone. Make sure that the driver, in their excitement over the arrival of their new vehicle, does not inadvertently sign a form showing damage to the old vehicle without realising. Some time later you will receive a bill for the damage from the supplier and a dispute will inevitably ensue.

Ideally when each vehicle is collected the fleet manager should carry out an inspection and sign the collection report. Bear in mind that if the car is dirty, the light is poor or the weather is bad it may be difficult for the condition of the vehicle to be assessed accurately.

The agreement will say the vehicle has to be returned at the end of the lease in good condition 'fair wear and tear for the age and mileage excepted'. The dividing line between fair wear and tear and unfair damage is set out in BVRLA Fair Wear and Tear Guide.

All contract hire agreements require you to insure the vehicle comprehensively and the supplier will normally ask for proof you have done this and paid the renewal premium.

Your 'leasing company' may not own the vehicle. They may be an intermediary (a small contract hire company or broker) acting as undisclosed agent for someone else. Ask who owns the vehicle. If the lessor's business collapses you may find yourself dealing with an organisation you have not heard of before.

The agreement may provide you with a **replacement vehicle** (a 'relief vehicle') if yours is off the road. It will specify; the circumstances in which the replacement will be provided (ie your vehicle is off the road after an accident, for servicing or either); the delay before it will be provided (eg 12, 24, 36, 48 hours); the period for which it can be used (eg 7, 14, 28 days etc) and the total number of days for which replacement vehicles will be supplied during the contract period.

In maintenance-inclusive contract hire the supplier will pay for the replacement of a fixed number of tyres, or for an unlimited number if you pay a little extra rental (though they won't pay for tyres damaged by bad driving). If a driver wears out more than the agreed number, try to find out why.

Whilst most vehicles on contract hire are supplied new, a few suppliers offer used vehicle contract hire. This can save you money and reduces the lessor's risk as they will not have to bear the huge depreciation that occurs when a new vehicle is driven out of the showroom door.

Contract hire offers you: Vehicle sourcing (no need for you to go out and find it); competitive interest rates within the rental (often lower than you would get if you searched the market for credit); the benefit of big fleet purchasing power; payment of all routine maintenance and servicing bills if you opt to include this (no need to scrutinise maintenance bills or negotiate with garages); automatic annual vehicle excise duty renewal (no need to go to the Post Office to renew); an off-balance sheet finance product; no residual value risk and no maintenance cost risk. There are some VAT benefits too. No wonder it's so popular.

The contract hire market is highly competitive. Many smaller companies simply shop around on a car-by-car basis to find the lowest quote and get their cars from a variety of suppliers.

The key is to find the organisation that will work the way you want. They may not offer the lowest price on a particular day but over time you are more likely to be happy with them.

Contract hire is a package of services and finance. In buying this package you give away some flexibility and control. You will notice this if you early terminate the lease or exceed the contract mileage. If you often have to change your vehicles at short notice, or are in a high staff-turnover business, you may find that early termination charges become burdensome. If you own your own vehicles you can do as you wish. For some, this is crucial.

OPERATING LEASE

An operating lease is one where the lessor retains substantially all of the risks and rewards of ownership. In practice, it is best to think of an operating lease as a simple rental agreement. You pay a rental then hand the asset back to the lessor. To recover their investment, they have to lease it to another party or sell it.

With an operating lease the supplier takes the residual value risk in the vehicle, so you do not have to show it on your balance sheet.

SALE AND LEASE BACK

With sale and lease back (often called 'purchase and lease back' or simply 'leaseback') you sell your vehicles to a lessor and continue to use them under the terms of a lease, usually contract hire. You might do this to raise cash, remove residual value risk, reduce administration or remove the vehicles from your balance sheet.

Sale and lease back is useful if you decide to use contract hire for the first time. You sell your existing fleet to the lessor so you can immediately start to enjoy the benefits of the supplier's service across your whole fleet.

FINANCE LEASE

A finance lease (also known as a 'full pay-out lease' or an 'open-ended' lease in the USA) transfers substantially all the risks and rewards of ownership of the asset to the lessee, putting them in much the same position as if they had bought the asset. The arrangement is similar to using one of the 'purchase' methods but the tax and accounting treatments are different.

The **primary period** is the initial non-cancellable period of the finance lease. During the **secondary period** the lessor allows you to continue leasing the vehicle until you both agree to end the lease or the vehicle is sold.

Normally with a finance lease there will be only one lessee. The lessor will charge you rentals that fully repay its investment during the primary period of the lease. You are committed to paying for at least this period and thereafter you will either sell the vehicle as the lessor's agent or opt to enter into a secondary lease period. On sale the lessor will allow you to keep most of the sale proceeds, which are normally paid as a rebate of rentals.

Finance leases often include a balloon rental at the end of the primary period. This reduces the monthly rentals you have to pay and can make them similar to the rentals in a contract hire agreement (though of course there is no balloon rental in contract hire).

Any secondary period rental will be tiny, perhaps a few percent of the cost of the vehicle. This '**peppercorn rental**' is normally paid annually and it is your ongoing acknowledgement that the vehicle is still under lease and you are not the owner.

In a finance lease you bear the risk of obsolescence of the vehicle. If it no longer suits your requirements you cannot hand it back mid-term without paying an early termination charge. You will be responsible for the maintenance of the vehicle unless you opt to include a maintenance package (as in contract hire).

As you are bearing the residual value risk on the vehicle, it has to be shown on your balance sheet.

Normally, the rentals remain fixed throughout the life of the lease, so you are not exposed to the risk of interest rates changing during this time.

Most lessees consider that finance leases have few advantages over contract hire. Hence finance leasing represents only 1% of the UK business vehicle finance market, down from 14% twenty years ago. However, in other countries (eg the USA) it is much more popular.

OPEN-BOOK LEASING

If you have a big fleet some contract hire companies will offer you a share of the profit they make in maintaining or selling your vehicles. They will send you initial information showing how your rentals have been calculated and then send you reports showing the financial performance of the lease, ie they will *open their books* to you.

They will make losses on some vehicles and these will be netted off against profits on others so that you only get the net profit, if any. The profit share calculation period is usually 12 months but for a big fleet it could be shorter to avoid building up big balances.

Heads you win, tails they lose. It makes you ask the question – how can they do it? It works for the leasing company because it normally gets them the right to be your sole supplier and ensures client loyalty. Also, open-book clients tend to look after their cars better because they have a vested interest in the return condition of the vehicles.

Open-book deals can be very valuable to lessees. They give you cheaper motoring and a good, close, long term relationship with a trusted supplier who will come to understand your business and will therefore be able to anticipate your needs.

SELECTING BETWEEN DIFFERENT METHODS OF FLEET FUNDING

As each business is different and has different priorities, internal resources, tax positions and so on, no one financial product is right for all businesses.

To determine the best way to fund your fleet you should consider: the overall cost of each method to your business (using discounted cash flow techniques to make these costs comparable); the balance sheet effect; the corporation tax effect; any relevant VAT issues; the employee benefit-in-kind tax issues; the flexibility you need; relevant human resource issues; risk management issues and internal administrative issues. Most of these are discussed in this book.

Such an exercise will allow you to focus on the products that work best for you. For many businesses several methods may be appropriate to cover different classes of vehicle or groups of employees.

LEASE V BUY

Should you buy a vehicle or lease it? To answer this question you need to consider whether you want to take the residual value risk, the tax effect if you buy rather than lease, and balance sheet issues. You will need also to carry out a financial evaluation of the lease v buy decision.

> You are about to acquire a new car. It costs £10,000 and you expect to sell it in three years' time for £3,000. You planned to buy it for cash but the salesman is offering you a non-maintenance contract hire deal at £2,800 per annum, payable annually in advance. The £10,000 would have come from your bank overdraft on which you currently pay interest at 10% per annum. Should you lease or buy?

You need a tool to help you make these comparisons and the best tool that we have is called **discounted cash flow analysis (DCF)**. DCF is a method of comparing alternative business options based on the cash flows they will produce and expressing these cash flows in today's money terms, the **present value (PV)**.

DCF uses the idea of the time value of money. £1 received in one year's time is worth less than £1 received today because you could invest £1 today to generate more over the year and also because inflation will reduce the value of that £1 over the year.

DCF uses interest rates to 'discount' (that is, to reduce) future cash flows to 'today's' value (the present value) so that they can then be added up or deducted as if they were all happening today. Then the present value of all of the cash flows of two competing options is compared and the option showing the highest present value (or the lowest negative present value) is the winner. See *Managing Your Company Cars* for worked examples.

DCF can help you decide whether to buy or use a lease, contract hire, contract purchase, hire purchase, lease purchase or a cash option, in fact for any situation where you have choices to make involving different cash flows.

CASH-RICH COMPANIES

'Cash-rich' companies have strong bank balances and no need to borrow. Many never consider leasing because they see it as a form of borrowing. Yet leasing can be attractive to these businesses because, unlike most businesses, leasing companies recover input VAT when buying vehicles to lease to their customers. Hence the rentals they charge are based on the capital cost before VAT.

In addition, contract hire is an off-balance sheet product and this may be an important factor for some cash-rich companies.

And finally, many cash-rich companies use fleet management products (eg purchasing, maintenance control, disposal, administration) as a way to outsource non-core activities and get the benefit of fleet discounts and expertise.

3 NEGOTIATE YOUR LEASE WISELY

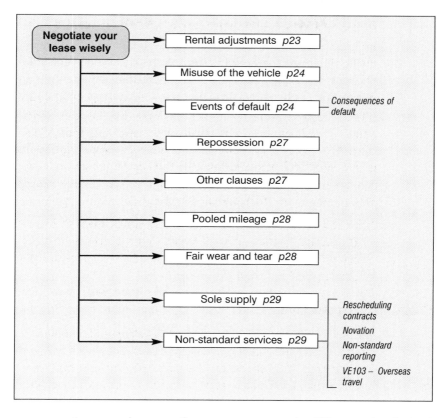

As every lease or finance agreement is different, the limited ambition of this chapter is to point out a few of the issues that you are likely to find in most vehicle leasing or finance agreements or that will arise during the life of the agreement. Praemonitus praemunitus! (Forewarned is forearmed).

RENTAL ADJUSTMENTS

The agreement will set out how rentals can be modified. There are several reasons why the lessor may wish to modify the rentals during the course of the agreement, the most common being when the list price of the vehicle changes between the date the contract is signed and the delivery date. Some manufacturers offer **price protection** so that price changes will not apply to vehicles that have already been ordered, but this is not universal, so the lessor needs to be able to alter the rentals before delivery to reflect this.

In large transactions it is normal to see a **tax variation clause**, giving the lessor the right to alter the rentals in the event of tax changes. When they calculate your rentals they assume they will get certain tax benefits including capital allowances and interest relief on borrowing costs. If the tax rules change, the lessor's return changes and a tax variation clause allows them to charge you more, even after the lease has ended, so they still earn the 'net of tax return' they originally expected to earn.

A good negotiation tactic is to point out to the lessor that any tax change might well benefit rather than disadvantage them and therefore you would be willing to retain the clause but want to make it two-way. So if the changes disadvantage the lessor you will accept extra charges; if they benefit the lessor you will get a refund.

Complex, protracted and very expensive court cases have been fought over tax variation clauses. It is important to make sure that you understand what the clause means if it appears in your agreement.

MISUSE OF THE VEHICLE

Unless specifically negotiated and included, leases will deny you the right to use a vehicle for racing, off-roading or carrying fare-paying passengers. You will be in breach of contract if you permit these and the agreement will make you responsible for any costs or losses that arise.

EVENTS OF DEFAULT

The contract may say the lessor will allow you uninterrupted use of the vehicle ('**quiet possession**') and will not interfere with your use of it, so long as you meet your obligations. You have this right automatically by law – it is an implied term of all lease agreements. However, if you fail to carry out certain obligations or actions set out in the agreement you will be deemed to be 'in default' of your obligations. The list of 'events of default' in a lease can be very long and the lessor will want the right to act promptly to protect themselves if something goes wrong with your business that could adversely affect them.

Many leases split events of default into different categories depending on the severity of the default, and allow the lessor different remedies for each category. So, for example, non-payment of a recharged parking fine might give the lessor the right to terminate the agreement after you have failed to make the payment within a reasonable time and they have given notice of their intention to terminate. At the other extreme, the bankruptcy or death of a sole trader or partner, or the convening of a meeting to appoint a liquidator or receiver, would normally bring the contract to an immediate end and give the lessor rights of immediate repossession.

CONSEQUENCES OF DEFAULT

If you are in default of your obligations the agreement will allow the lessor to recover ('repossess') the vehicle by entering your premises if necessary and to charge interest on late payment at a default rate.

The contract will set out how the lessor will calculate the sum payable on default. This amount, the **'termination sum'**, guarantees the lessor will cover the balance outstanding in its books on termination. It will include any loss, costs or expenses the lessor incurs in repossessing or collecting the vehicle, legal costs and arrears. All future rentals that would have been payable had the lease continued normally will also be payable, subject to a discount for early payment expressed as an annual interest rate, for example '5% per annum'. This does not mean that the amount payable will be the future rentals less 5%. The 'per annum' part here is important, as it is a discounted cash flow concept that means that the rental payable in twenty-four months' time will be discounted more heavily than the rental payable in 12 months' time.

The rate of interest the lessor charges you on late payment may be higher than their normal rate of interest but cannot be a randomly determined figure designed to penalise you. They can charge '**liquidated damages**' (a justifiable amount; their reasonable estimate of their additional costs once you have gone into default) but not a '**penalty**' (an arbitrary charge). The courts will not enforce a penalty.

You will usually be required to pay the termination sum immediately and the lessor will later refund the net proceeds received from selling the vehicle. In practice, however, if the lessor recovers and sells the vehicle promptly, you will only be charged the termination sum less the net sale proceeds of the vehicle.

If you have a disagreement with your lessor you can try to resolve it amicably. The next step might be to make a complaint to the appropriate trade body, perhaps the BVRLA or the Finance and Leasing Association (FLA). Or you could take the dispute to court. However, the Arbitration Act provides an alternative way to resolve disputes – **arbitration**. Many leases allow disputes to be resolved in this way, and allow the President of the BVRLA to appoint the arbitrator. The Act covers only England and Wales: Scotland has its own procedures that are beyond the scope of this book.

If you and the lessor agree to refer the dispute to arbitration, an independent third party will be appointed to look at the evidence, hear the cases of the parties (represented by lawyers if they wish) and make a judgement. This decision is binding on both parties. You cannot back out of the process and ignore the judgement if it goes against you.

Normally the costs of the arbitration are borne by the 'loser'. However, if party A makes an offer to settle the dispute which party B rejects, and B subsequently wins the case but is awarded less than A's original offer, B will have to pay the costs arising after the offer was made. Generally, arbitration is a cheaper and quicker method of dispute resolution than going to court. The arbitrator will normally be an expert in the matter under dispute, unlike a judge.

Repossession

In most finance agreements and leases the finance company/lessor remains the owner of the vehicle and has a right to repossess and sell it if the client goes into default. However, in a credit sale agreement there is no such clear-cut right, as title to the vehicle passes to the borrower at the start of the agreement. In these situations the lender will have to rely on some other form of security, usually a guarantee from the borrower's employer.

If the car has been sold by the borrower/lessee without the consent of the lender/lessor, the rules are complicated. If a car is bought by a private individual acting in good faith (ie they fully believed they were buying it from someone who had the right to sell it), the buyer gets good title and the car cannot be repossessed.

However, if it was bought by a private individual who was not acting in good faith (ie they knew or should reasonably have been expected to know the seller had no right to sell it), the buyer does not get good title and the finance company/lessor has the right to repossess it from the buyer.

Other clauses

All finance agreements require you to pay on the due date and include a clause saying that **'time is of the essence'**. Pay late and you risk running up large interest charges, the suspension of maintenance services (for maintenance-inclusive contracts) or the repossession of the vehicles – or all three.

Most lessors require payment by **direct debit** for all but the largest clients. If you insist on paying by cheque you may find the lessor loses interest in supplying you.

The contract will say whether the agreement is to be governed by the law in England and Wales, or Scotland, or some other jurisdiction. Scottish contract law differs in some regards from English and Welsh law. For example, in Scotland there is a requirement for contracts to be witnessed by two parties.

POOLED MILEAGE

Rather than charging you for excess mileage at Xp per mile and giving no credit for under-mileage, the mileages of all your vehicles that terminate in a 'pooling period' can be aggregated and compared with the aggregate of their contractual mileages.

If there is a net excess you will be charged for this or possibly allowed to carry ('roll') the excess miles forward into the next pooling period. If there is a net credit (ie you have driven less than the contracted aggregate mileage) you will be allowed to carry this forward to the next pooling period or possibly receive a refund.

Some lessors give less credit for under-mileage than they charge for over-mileage, arguing that if one vehicle has travelled 5,000 miles in excess of the contract mileage and another has travelled 5,000 miles below the contract mileage, the reduction in sale proceeds and increased maintenance spend on the high-mileage vehicle will be greater than the increase in sale proceeds on the low mileage vehicle.

Pooling periods may be of any length but quarterly, six-monthly and annual are common. Quarterly pooling probably works best for larger fleets, where many vehicles will come off lease every quarter.

FAIR WEAR AND TEAR

In requiring you to return the vehicle to the lessor in good condition, 'fair wear and tear excepted', the agreement leaves a great deal open to interpretation. BVRLA members comply with the BVRLA Fair Wear and Tear Guide. However, while this publication may reduce misunderstandings, it cannot say whether you should be charged £50 or £155 for a particular scratch. To avoid disputes over small amounts of damage, some lessors set a de minimis level (perhaps £100) below which you will not be charged for damage to the vehicle (a '**damage waiver**' limit). Damage above this amount is then charged to you in full.

It is worthwhile shopping around to find the contract hire company that will give you the highest damage waiver limit, particularly if your current supplier charges for damage on a high proportion of the cars you return.

SOLE SUPPLY

Here you agree to place all of your vehicle finance and/or management requirements with one supplier.

There are many advantages to a sole supply agreement. You will have only one point of contact to meet all your needs and you can develop a partnership with that organisation. They then have the incentive to deliver a high quality proactive service, for if they were to fail they would lose all your business.

Sole supply contract hire allows all your vehicles to be grouped together for pooled mileage purposes. If they were split between two suppliers, you might have to pay excess mileage charges to one without being able to access a large credit balance with the other.

Sole supply gives you just one set of reports to review: There is no need for you to consolidate information from several sources.

The main disadvantage of sole supply is that you may lose out on the benefits of competitive pricing. Suppliers tend to offer keener prices if they know they are in a competitive position. However you can still check your supplier's prices against their competitors' from time to time, to keep them on their toes.

NON-STANDARD SERVICES

During the life of the agreement you may need to ask the lessor to perform services that are not mentioned in the contract. Most contract hire companies will accommodate any reasonable request, though some will make a charge for these.

RESCHEDULING CONTRACTS

Most leasing companies will allow you to change the term and mileage of the contract to reduce the rentals but will not be too keen if you keep on asking for the rentals to be changed again and again. Eventually they will begin to talk of charging you for this service. They will not charge a lot, perhaps £75, but this means you will think twice about asking for further changes.

The better contract hire companies will proactively advise you if your vehicles are running at well under or over the contracted mileage. They will be keen for you to reschedule so as not to build up nasty shocks for either party at the end of the contract.

NOVATION

This is a legal agreement entered into between three parties that relates to an earlier contract between two of them. Novations often arise when an employee resigns and wants to take their company car to a new employer who is willing to take over the lease. In the novation agreement the three parties agree to restart the lease as if the 'old' employer was never involved in the contract and the new employer had been the lessee from day 1. This benefits everyone; the old employer avoids an early termination charge, the new employer inherits a shorter lease and the lessor has a new client.

Most lessors will permit a novation to take place if they are satisfied about the creditworthiness of the new employer.

NON-STANDARD REPORTING

All contract hire companies provide reports to their clients. At their most basic these reports include lists of vehicles soon to come off lease or soon to require an MOT.

Some suppliers will routinely produce exception reports to show you which vehicles are running at particularly high or low mileage rates compared with the original contract mileages.

The contract hire company holds a lot of information about your fleet and drivers and they can produce tailored reports for you, either routinely or on an ad-hoc basis. They are normally happy to do this for free although if you start to use a lot of their internal resource they may charge a small fee.

VE103 Vehicle on Hire Certificate for overseas travel

If you want to take a leased vehicle abroad you must obtain a certificate confirming the owner has consented. A letter from the owner is insufficient for this purpose.

A special VE103 certificate is required and only a handful of bodies in the UK (eg AA, RAC) can issue these. The leasing company buys blank VE103s from an issuing body to give to you, and most will levy a small charge for doing so.

4 CHOOSE THE RIGHT SERVICES

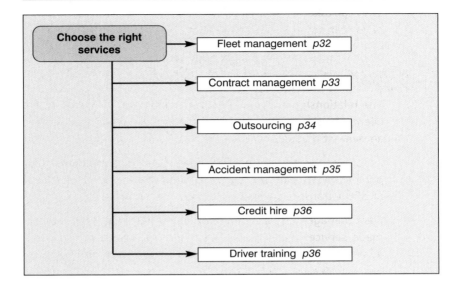

Choose the right services
- Fleet management *p32*
- Contract management *p33*
- Outsourcing *p34*
- Accident management *p35*
- Credit hire *p36*
- Driver training *p36*

FLEET MANAGEMENT

This term describes the services a contract hire or fleet management company can provide you that do not involve funding. These include vehicle purchase, maintenance control, invoice checking, vehicle excise duty renewal, vehicle disposal, accident management, provision of replacement vehicles, breakdown cover arrangements, management reporting, dealing with parking and speeding fines, etc. The service is usually fee-based, and many companies find these fees to be very good value for money.

A fleet management service gives you access to the supplier's expertise and economies of scale. They manage thousands of vehicles and buy vehicles and services efficiently and cost-effectively. They will authorise necessary maintenance work, dispose of vehicles efficiently, get the right sale price and deal with all the day-to-day administrative matters that arise in the management of a fleet. They are set up to do this; experts handle each part of the process.

They can take the residual value and maintenance risks or you can, or you can agree a **'risks and rewards sharing'** arrangement. If you offer them an incentive to achieve the highest disposal price (perhaps a share of any sale proceeds received in excess of CAP Clean plus X%) this can work well for you both.

The relationship between a fleet management company and its client is usually very close and it is important to have an agreement that sets out very clearly who will do what.

If your contract says the fleet management company is your purchase agent they are legally required to give you full details of all of the transactions they enter into on your behalf.

Fleet management is suitable for large fleets that need a tailor-made service, medium size businesses that want to outsource administrative functions, and cash-rich companies that buy their own vehicles and need administrative support. Smaller companies tend to buy contract hire rather than fleet management.

Whilst suppliers can offer you lots of fleet management services and will tailor them to your needs, do consider whether you really need a tailor made solution. As in most areas of business, made-to-measure is usually much cheaper than tailor-made. If it works for everyone else do you really need to ask the supplier to bend their standard service to meet your needs?

CONTRACT MANAGEMENT

Here you buy a maintenance package from the supplier for a fixed monthly price. The package typically includes all the items that would normally be included in a maintenance-inclusive contract hire agreement, including road tax renewal. The advantage of contract management is that you pay a fixed price and they take the risk on the actual level of costs.

Contract management is useful if you want to fix your running costs and either buy your cars outright or fund them with a purchase method of finance such as lease purchase.

OUTSOURCING

This is one of the most widely used terms in the vehicle management market and everyone has their own understanding of what it means. At its simplest, it means asking a third party to carry out some functions you previously handled in-house, and paying them a fee. The supplier usually allocates dedicated support staff and provides detailed reports so you can monitor what is happening.

Many functions can be outsourced to a contract hire or fleet management company. For example, vehicle purchasing, maintenance invoice checking, parking fine administration, fuel management, vehicle disposal, driver contact, accident management and query handling.

If you have a very large fleet, this arrangement may include the use of '**inplants**' – members of the supplier's staff who work in your office and manage the day-to-day functions of the contract. (Interesting to note that 'inplant' does not appear in any dictionary).

In some senses contract hire is outsourcing because it encompasses many of the fleet management functions you would otherwise have to carry out yourself.

Outsourcing can offer many benefits. It can reduce (or fix) your costs, reduce your risks, increase efficiency and be more flexible than in-house solutions, giving you access to better systems and purchasing power and allowing you to focus on your core business.

Unless implemented carefully, outsourcing can involve a loss of control. For example, if you outsource the authorisation of maintenance expenditure, someone other than you will be deciding how to spend your money.

When one of your drivers has an accident there can be a lot of work involved in processing the claim and getting the vehicle back on the road. An accident management service takes this work from you and puts it into the hands of specialists.

Accident management (also known as **insurance claims management**) is available from contract hire, fleet management or specialist accident management companies. It is normally a fee-based service.

The supplier takes over from the moment of impact and handles the whole process until the claim has been finalised. They arrange to remove the damaged vehicle from the road, inspect the damage, obtain quotes for repair, accept the best quote, inspect the completed work, pay the repairer, handle claims paperwork, provide a replacement vehicle or courtesy car and handle correspondence with the other side's insurer. The main emphasis of the service is to get your driver back on the road as quickly as possible.

If you have an accident and it is not your fault, some of your expenses may have to be recovered from the other party or their insurer. These could include legal fees, your insurance excess and any out of pocket expenses not covered by your insurance. So **uninsured loss recovery** is normally offered as part of the accident management service.

Accident management companies normally control costs by using a network of approved repairers. Some charge low fees and earn most of their income by adding a premium to the actual repair and car hire costs. This can give the supplier a conflict of interest because the more the work costs, the more they make. So check how your supplier plans to earn their income and decide if you are happy with this.

Professional accident management takes away a large administrative task and puts it into the hands of specialists. You benefit from nationally agreed labour rates for repairs and will receive regular management reports to keep you up-to-date with what is happening with each claim.

Whoever is to blame for the accident, it is usually a relief for the driver to hand over control to an expert who is emotionally detached.

Every accident involves a lot of administration. However, one important asset needs to be considered first – the driver. If one of your drivers has been involved in an accident they may be injured, upset, annoyed, traumatised, confused, disorientated, feeling guilty or angry.

Make sure they are ok and that their needs have been taken care of before you get them involved in the admin. They may have done no more than scraped the car whilst driving out of the office car park. At the other extreme they may have been in an accident where someone was killed or seriously injured, perhaps a loved one. You may be the first person in your business that they have spoken to, and the accident may have happened only a few minutes ago. The employee may need hospitalisation, the attention of a doctor or nurse, counselling or time off. If you have a human resources manager, make them aware that one of your employees has been involved in a serious accident and advise the employee's manager too.

CREDIT HIRE

Most insurance policies give you the right to a courtesy car when your car is off the road after an accident. If the accident was not your fault you can ask a credit hire company to supply a vehicle to you at no cost. They reclaim their hire charges from your insurance company.

DRIVER TRAINING

We all have to be trained and to pass a driving test before being allowed to drive. Then we tear up our L-plates and are let out onto the roads. However, over time, we can pick up bad driving habits that go unremarked.

Many employers have come to realise that their drivers need ongoing training if they are to be expected to drive safely for the company and to look after themselves and other road users.

Driver training companies offer courses to suit all needs and budgets. The 'standard' fleet driver course focuses on **defensive driving**. The idea is that other drivers may drive badly but so long as you drive well you can minimise the possibility of accidents.

These companies can provide a classroom-based training session for all of your drivers in one morning, offering insights into the reasons why accidents happen and making your drivers think about their own driving style. These sessions are followed by on-the-road training: A qualified driving instructor takes the wheel and points out the steps he is taking to ensure the journey is as safe as possible without compromising the need to arrive at the destination as quickly as possible. Your driver then takes over the wheel and the instructor points out the good aspects of their driving and those that could benefit from being changed.

Also available are skid training, motorway driving courses, off-road courses, post-accident counselling and courses tailored to your specific needs.

A good approach is to send drivers for training in groups according to the level of risk they are exposed to. For example, groups of high mileage drivers, or those with poor accident records, might be the first to receive training.

The insurance industry and the driver training industry have statistics showing that trained drivers have significantly fewer accidents. This leads to lower repair bills, less vehicle downtime and reduced driver stress.

5 UNDERSTAND CASH ALLOWANCES

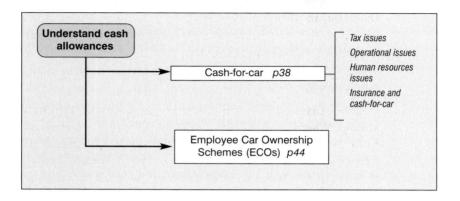

CASH-FOR-CAR

In concept, a cash-for-car scheme is very simple: Your employee gives up their company car and the company pays them more salary, a '**cash allowance**'.

Increasing levels of benefit-in-kind tax in recent years have disadvantaged many company car drivers. For some, the tax they pay exceeds the cost they would incur if they simply took extra salary from their employer and acquired their own car. And some employers have always believed the administration of a company car fleet is an unnecessary burden.

If one of your employees takes extra salary in lieu of a company car, they fall outside the benefit-in-kind income tax regime. This saves you having to pay the employer's Class 1A National Insurance contributions. Employees who take cash allowances and still need vehicles in order to do their jobs then have to provide these themselves. They fund this using their increased salary and a mileage allowance for each business mile they drive.

Many employers give their staff the option to take extra salary In lieu of a company car.

There are several possible cash-for-car arrangements. A few employers have downgraded the value of the car on offer and simultaneously given their employees a cash offer to induce them to opt out of the company car. Some have introduced **employer-sponsored personal contract purchase schemes**, and introduced their staff to a leasing company that provides fully maintained cars under PCP contracts. Others have introduced **employee car ownership schemes (ECOs)** (*see page 44*). And some have stopped providing cars altogether, given extra salary and left the employees to get on with it.

In some cases cash-for-car schemes can generate significant savings. Where this happens you need to decide who will benefit from these. If the company keeps all the savings you may find it hard to encourage employees to opt out of their company cars. If the savings are shared between the company and the employees this may encourage take-up but may not be ideal for the company's bottom line.

It makes sense to work with a leasing company to introduce a cash-for-car scheme. You are not giving an employee several thousand pounds cash to buy a car; you are giving them a monthly allowance and they need a way to convert that into mobility. A lease or PCP allows them to do this and if you set up a scheme with a leasing company you can make sure your employees receive the right deal.

Tax issues

Whilst generally this book excludes tax issues, tax is a central consideration with cash-for-car schemes so some general comments are appropriate here.

You have to be certain that moving to a cash option would be the best move for your business. The calculations are complex. Explaining them to a single driver is time-consuming but for a large group it is daunting. Consultants have earned a great deal introducing these schemes to companies.

In extremis, there are likely to be significant savings if a higher rate taxpaying company car driver who drives high business mileage in a high-CO_2 car can be encouraged to take a cash allowance and give up their company car. The benefits reduce as the tax rate, level of business mileage and emissions levels reduce.

A badly set up cash-for-car scheme may fail to remove the benefit-in-kind tax charge from an employee. Several schemes have failed to pass the Inland Revenue's tests and you are strongly advised to clear the scheme with the Inland Revenue.

If you offer cash instead of a company car, you will not have to pay Class 1A National Insurance contributions. Any cash allowance paid to the employee will be fully taxable at the employee's marginal rate of tax. You will pay Class 1 employer's National Insurance contributions and most employees will pay Class 1 NIC on the cash allowance.

You will need to pay a mileage allowance to an employee who uses his or her private vehicle on company business. This can be any amount you agree with the employee and will be tax-free for the employee so long as it does not exceed the Inland Revenue **Approved Mileage Allowance Payment (AMAP)** levels. If the employee is paid less than the AMAP rate they can claim tax relief on the shortfall. If the payment exceeds the AMAP levels, the excess will be taxable at the employee's marginal tax rate.

If you wish to adopt a cash-for-car scheme, it makes sense to pay the employee the full amount of the AMAP (as it is tax- and NIC-free) and a lower level of cash allowance (which would be fully taxable).

You may give your employees interest-free or low interest loans of up to £5,000, tax-free, to help them buy their own vehicles. They can use these as a deposit towards a lease agreement and this will reduce their monthly payments to the funder/lessor.

You need to give very careful consideration to setting up a cash-for-car scheme and also decide whether any savings should be kept by the company or shared with the employees. In recent years there has been a growth in ECO schemes that move employees en masse out of company cars and into cars they own themselves. These are designed to remove the car from the company car tax regime and can provide some of the tax savings mentioned above.

Further tax information is available from many sources, including the HM Revenue and Customs website www.hmrc.gov.uk.

OPERATIONAL ISSUES

Selecting, test-driving, buying, maintaining, insuring, arranging roadside recovery and disposing of a car all cause hassle. With company cars the employer has the hassle but with many cash-for-car arrangements it is left with the employee.

As well as making complex calculations when implementing your cash-for-car scheme, you will have to make some important policy decisions.

In many company car schemes, employees are allowed to select a car from a list according to the employee's grade within the company. When introducing cash-for-car schemes, many employers have tried to replace these car bands with cash bands – "if you are at such-and-such a grade you are entitled to receive £400 per month instead of a company car" – and have encountered a major complication. If two employees earn the same salary and do the same job but drive different levels of business mileage, paying them the same cash allowance and the same mileage allowance will leave one substantially better off than the other: One may be unable to afford the same car as the other. So, by and large, cash bands can prove problematic in cash-for-car schemes.

The scheme also needs to say what happens if a driver changes job inside the organisation and consequently no longer drives the same business mileage. Who pays the additional costs or benefits from the savings, the employer or the employee?

Vehicle selection has been an issue in some schemes. Most employers are used to stipulating the type, age and quality of car that can be used on company business (eg no convertibles, nothing over four years old, etc). However, in a cash allowance scheme employees feel they should be able to use their money however they want, so thousands have chosen cars they could never have driven previously, or selected quality used vehicles to stretch their cash allowance further. The tide is now turning again because of the new focus on fleet safety, so more cash-for-car fleets are now restricting the cars that can be used for business purposes.

As already stated, determining the cash allowance to pay the employee is a complex calculation. Many employers think they can pay a monthly allowance equal to the contract hire rental they had previously paid for the employee's car but in many cases once this has been added to the employee's salary and taxed, the employee has not had enough left to lease a car. And for a cash-for-car scheme to work effectively the employee needs to have a good idea of the level of business mileage they will drive – yet many don't.

If your employees use their own cars on company business, the cars must comply with health and safety legislation, be properly maintained, roadworthy and insured for business. These cars should be included in your health and safety risk assessments.

HUMAN RESOURCE ISSUES

There is a disagreement on how employees can be encouraged to take up cash-for-car schemes. Some consultants insist that all employees can be pushed into them on the same day without any problems. Others disagree.

If your company's employment contract says you will provide the employee with a specific car or its equivalent, you must do so. You cannot unilaterally withdraw this benefit. If it says you can change this benefit at your sole discretion, you are free to make whatever changes you wish, though you may then have an exceptionally unhappy workforce. To avoid staff dissatisfaction most good employers have consulted their staff and tried to encourage them to relinquish their cars in favour of cash.

Faced with the withdrawal of their company vehicles, employees are rarely enthusiastic. Once their company car goes, many will have to enter into finance agreements involving a commitment to pay thousands of pounds over a number of years.

This raises a number of issues. If they have concerns about job security (for example, if they have received a poor staff appraisal or the company has made people redundant recently) they may be reluctant to enter into such an obligation. If they are planning to move home they may be worried what the lender will say on seeing several thousand pounds of additional debt. When the cash-for-car scheme is first introduced, employees may calculate that they benefit from the cash allowance. However, if they later change jobs internally and drive fewer business miles, this can make them worse off than if they had kept a company car. Maternity leave or illness may keep the driver off the road for several months but the lease payments on the car will still have to be made.

Gross salary is normally the starting point for calculating some employee benefits such as pension contributions (in defined contribution schemes), so most cash-for-car schemes say the cash allowance shall be excluded when calculating pension benefits.

Cash-for-car schemes can be good for companies with flat grading structures as these schemes do away with overt status symbols.

In summary, cash-for-car schemes can be motivational. They can allow the individual employee quite a lot of freedom in selecting their own vehicle and save money. However, introduced incorrectly they can expose your drivers to financial risks and have a demotivating effect. They expose the company to health and safety risks that may be hard to control. Indeed, the trend away from company cars seems to have reversed in the last few years because of fleet safety concerns.

INSURANCE AND CASH-FOR-CAR

When cash allowance schemes first became popular insurance proved problematic. Employees do not build up no-claims bonuses while driving company cars and some opted for cash allowances and were then quoted large premiums by motor insurers that did not recognise their years of accident-free motoring. Insurers have since recognised the opportunities arising from the cash-for-car trend and this is no longer such a problem.

Fierce competition in the private motor insurance market since the arrival of the 'direct insurers' has driven down the cost of private motor insurance. It is now much cheaper than fleet cover and if you own a small fleet you may be tempted to ask your employees to arrange cover in their own names rather than have a company insurance policy. This is a very bad idea: If someone is seriously injured when your employee is driving under a business policy, the policy protects your business against any claims. However, if the employee is the insured party – ie if they only have private motor insurance – the business has no such protection and is exposed to the full cost of any claim by the employee or third party, even if the driver was insured to drive the car for business purposes. And if the employee leaves the company they take their no-claims bonus with them.

You should give your drivers guidance on what to do in the event of an accident. Your insurer can provide a written procedure that you can customise to your own company's situation. The driver should complete an accident report form; yours, the insurer's or both.

Around 60% of companies charge employees who cause an accident in a company vehicle. 25% charge the employee for every incident, the remainder charge only if the driver has been responsible for more than one accident in a twelve-month period. The amounts vary but most charge an amount equal to the excess on the insurance policy.

If you plan to charge your drivers who cause an accident, it is important to have a written company policy and to make sure all drivers are aware of this.

Employee Car Ownership Schemes (ECOs)

These are employer-sponsored schemes designed to reduce the overall tax burden of providing cars to employees. Some organisations call these **Employee Car Ownership Plans (ECOPs), Structured Leasing Schemes** or **Structured Car Purchase Schemes**.

These schemes are based on credit sale agreements so title in the vehicle passes immediately to the employee at the inception of the agreement. Company car benefit-in-kind tax only applies where a car is made available by reason of the employee's employment and where title to the vehicle has not passed to the employee. So a scheme where title passes to the employee is outside the scope of benefit-in-kind tax.

This does not mean that it will avoid taxation completely, just the company car benefit-in-kind tax. There are many hurdles to trip the unwary, and parts of any such scheme may cause other taxable benefits to arise.

ECOs are complex to set up and require ongoing management and tax consultancy. They can be very expensive too. Fleets with a few hundred vehicles have been asked to pay set-up consultancy fees exceeding £100,000.

These schemes work by giving the employee a cash allowance. This needs to be amended if there is a change in corporation tax rates, NIC rates, AMAP rates, the mileage the driver is covering or their marginal income tax rate.

ECOs are generally unsuited to companies with high levels of staff turnover.

The Inland Revenue has confirmed that no special tax charge will be levied on properly-established ECO schemes. They are willing to pre-approve ECO schemes – a sensible precaution for any employer. You are strongly advised not to change an established ECO scheme without going back to the Inland Revenue to get the changes approved.

There is a parallel to be drawn between an ECO scheme and a final salary pension scheme: The employer takes on an open-ended risk on both.

In summary, if correctly established, an ECO scheme can give an employee all the benefits of a company car while the employer, and possibly also the employee, saves money. However, these schemes are costly to set up, require long term assistance and consultancy from external experts and require reworking every time there is a change in tax rates or rules.

If you are keen to explore these schemes, the message is the same as with any other major change: Shop around, do your research, involve all interested parties within your business (purchasing, human resources, finance, legal) and only proceed when you are sure it will benefit your business.

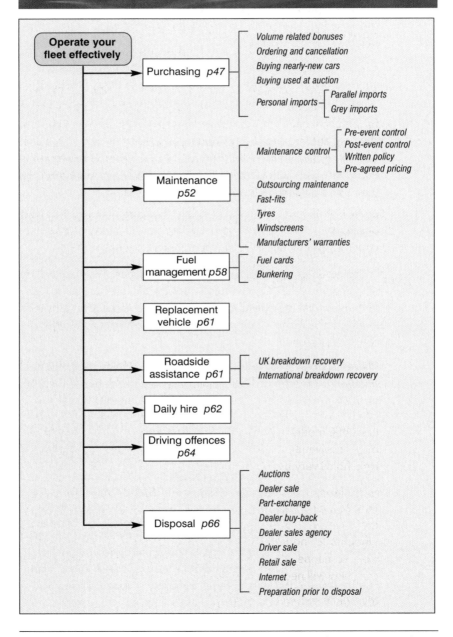

Many smaller businesses allow their employees to find, test-drive and order their own company cars.

However, buying the occasional vehicle from different dealers means spreading your buying power around, rather than concentrating it.

And allowing employees to order their cars may not impress your auditors: unscrupulous employees can manipulate the transaction for personal gain, for example selling their spouse's car as part of the deal and getting a great trade-in price for that car at the cost of a lower discount on the new car. A far better approach is to nominate one dealer for each make of vehicles and negotiate a standard discount off the manufacturer's list price.

Even if you have a very small fleet you can still get big fleet purchasing power by taking a car on lease from a contract hire company or buying through a fleet management company.

Volume related bonuses

One of the unusual features of the motor industry is that fleet buyers can get two discounts; one from the dealer and another from the manufacturer.

Manufacturers give discounts ('**volume related bonuses**' or '**VRBs**') to organisations that buy large numbers of vehicles, for example contract hire companies and large corporates. The level of VRB is normally determined by a series of thresholds; eg buy 25 units of a model and you may receive £200 per vehicle, buy 50 you may receive £500 per vehicle, and so on. The amounts and thresholds vary by make and model and change over time.

Alternatively, some manufacturers offer '**specific support**' (special bonuses) for individual customers. Whilst it is hard to generalise on these deals, it is fair to say that manufacturers will pay large amounts to induce the largest fleets to buy their product rather than someone else's. Your contract hire or fleet management company will negotiate to obtain these on your behalf.

Manufacturers will not provide VRBs on parallel imports.

ORDERING AND CANCELLATION

Always place your orders in writing, using your own standard order form. By using your own form you reduce the chance of ordering the wrong vehicle – potentially a very expensive mistake.

If you cancel an order you may be asked to pay a cancellation fee. A long chain of actions will have been put in motion to get you the car you require and the supplier will have gone to some expense. If you cancel after the dealer has registered the vehicle, they may well be left holding a vehicle built to your specification that they cannot sell. Once registered this becomes a used vehicle. The dealer can deregister it at the DVLA but this is a hassle and the DVLA can refuse to deregister a vehicle that has been delivered to a customer.

If you cancel an order you placed with a contract hire company, either the dealer, the contract hire company or both may charge a cancellation fee unless you cancelled because the price of the vehicle increased.

BUYING NEARLY-NEW CARS

Most fleets buy only new cars. There are various reasons for this. It is reassuring to have the full benefit of the manufacturer's warranty, it is easy to find the car you are looking for, there are no doubts about the history of the car, the mileage will be negligible (and verifiably so), and the driver will get the nice warm feeling that comes from having a brand new car.

However, you pay a huge premium for a new vehicle. There are plenty of situations where a company could make do with a quality used car instead. Newly recruited or promoted employees, staff on secondment, staff requiring a car temporarily, pool cars – in all these situations a used car would be an acceptable alternative.

A well-maintained twelve-month-old car is the same car as it was twelve months earlier, with the same specification, performance, fuel consumption and CO_2 output – but it is 20-30% cheaper to buy.

If you buy a used vehicle at a dealer it comes with the dealer's warranty and maybe also the unexpired portion of the manufacturer's warranty. But if you buy from a dealer you will also be paying the dealer's mark-up.

If you buy a used car from a small dealer or a private individual, check its provenance. If you are unsure of its age or description call the **DVLA's premium rate phone line** (0906 185 8585) to check its first registration date and engine size. You can check the **HPI database** to see if it has been stolen, written-off, clocked or has outstanding finance (www.hpicheck.com)

Whilst your financial director may want you to choose used cars, your human resource director will argue that a used car will be less appealing to your employees, imply a loss of status and may affect staff motivation and recruitment.

BUYING USED AT AUCTION

You can pick up a real bargain if you buy a used car at an auction. Contract hire companies sell ex-lease cars at auction because of the speed and efficiency of the process. Their cars are normally two to four years old, properly maintained and come with a full maintenance history.

Each auction house offers a range of sales. There are sales for 'Top Cars' (executive cars), classic cars, sales by named contract hire companies and general sales. You can find out what sales are coming up by looking at auction houses' websites and can see what cars are being sold by phoning the auction house for a list or using their faxback service. When you go to an auction you need to have a good idea of what you are looking for and the price you want to pay. You will be lost without a copy of one of the published trade price guides the professional traders use, **CAP Black Book** (www.cap.co.uk) or **Glass's Guide** (www.glass.co.uk).

If you buy at auction you must pay for the vehicle when the hammer falls, unless you have pre-agreed a credit facility with the auction house.

Personal imports

These are advertised in the Sunday newspapers and in the back of motoring magazines.

There are two broad classes of personal import – parallel and grey.

Parallel imports

Under European Union law you can buy your new car anywhere in the EU. Some UK businesses will buy a car for you on the Continent and deliver it to your door. In some cases significant savings can be obtained, even after you have paid for delivery, customs clearance and VAT.

You can wait longer for a right-hand drive car ordered from the Continent than from the UK.

Many UK cars are now supplied with three-year warranties. Typically, the first year is provided by the manufacturer, the next two by the dealer. Normally, if you buy on the Continent you will only get a one-year warranty.

As parallel imports are EU-specification cars, there should be no problems on resale of the vehicle, but used car buyers are conservative and may well mark down the value of a parallel import simply because it is 'different'.

It is illegal for a manufacturer to obstruct you if you buy a new car elsewhere in the EU or to cause problems for you once the car is in the UK.

For so long as the UK remains outside the Euro zone the relative attractiveness of parallel imports will always depend on the Sterling-Euro exchange rate.

Most contract hire companies will not buy or finance parallel imports.

Grey imports

These are cars bought outside the EU and imported to the UK without going through the manufacturer's normal distribution channels.

Most of the world drives on the right hand side of the road. The exceptions are some former British possessions (India, Australia,

Pakistan, etc) and, notably, Japan. Cars are cheaper in many of these countries and in recent years large numbers of used cars have been imported from these countries.

Many problems have been reported with grey imports. As some of these cars are not built to UK specification, some owners have had difficulty obtaining spare parts or insurance quotes.

Lessors are reluctant to buy these cars because sale of goods and consumer protection laws oblige them to give the customer an implied warranty as to the merchantability of the vehicle. In many cases lessors are unable to verify whether a car is fit to be driven on the UK highway.

Finally and crucially, lessors have been worried about whether they were getting '**good title**' (proper legal ownership) to the vehicle in the first place. When a vehicle's original registration and subsequent sale documents are in Japanese, life becomes difficult for lessors. There have been thousands of cases of right-hand drive vehicles being stolen to order in Japan, transported on containers to the Middle East, given false papers and then shipped to the UK for sale to unsuspecting buyers. This was the subject of a detailed BBC TV 'Panorama' investigation. Where a stolen vehicle is acquired the buyer cannot get good title and many innocent UK buyers of these vehicles have had their cars impounded by the police. Hence motor industry insiders are wary of buying these vehicles.

If despite these issues you decide to buy a grey import, do your research thoroughly. Check to see how much it differs from the UK model and make sure you buy from a reputable dealer.

The **British Independent Motor Traders Association (BIMTA)** provides services for people buying imported vehicles, including a money-back guarantee if the vehicle turns out to have been registered as stolen prior to export from Japan. (www.bimta.com).

If you decide to import a vehicle personally you must notify HM Customs Central Processing Unit within seven days of bringing it into the country and give them the purchase invoice and Appendix D of Customs form 728. They will calculate the VAT due, which must be paid within 30 days, and you will then receive a customs clearance form 386 to send to the DVLA to register the vehicle.

Maintenance Control

Few fleets have their own servicing facilities. Many rely on local dealerships, fast-fits and repair shops to meet their service, maintenance and repair (SMR) needs. Others prefer to delegate these arrangements to contract hire or fleet management companies

In many small businesses the driver decides their vehicle requires servicing or repair work, then takes it in to a convenient garage, gets the work done, pays the bill and claims the cost back on expenses.

You may encounter problems if you adopt this approach. Your driver may forget to have routine servicing work or MoT tests carried out when due, or may pay too much for the work. The garage may say that a piece of work is necessary or a part needs to be fitted, when an alternative, cheaper option is available.

There are no economies of scale here: The dealer might have offered you a discount had they known they would be getting in more than one car for servicing or repair. And you have no control over the driver's actions: they may ask for work to be done simply because they feel it would be nice to have, rather than it being essential for the function or safety of the vehicle.

Many companies allow their drivers to buy their company cars when these are de-fleeted. Unscrupulous drivers can ask for additional work to be done to the car at the company's expense just before they buy it ('**pre-conditioning**').

So giving your employees full control of the maintenance of their vehicles is unlikely to be in the best interests of your business.

The key elements of managing maintenance expenditure are pre- and post-event control, written maintenance policies, pre-agreed pricing structures and warranty claims.

Pre-event control

This is a management process whereby a qualified, authorised person receives a quote for SMR work and decides whether or not to accept it. To make the right decision they need access to the maintenance history of the vehicle. If they accept the quote they issue an order number and record this on the maintenance record.

The maintenance record can be quite basic and many small fleets simply keep a file to log each event that happens to the car, showing the date, cost and brief details of the work.

Post-event control

Post-event control involves checking suppliers' invoices against the maintenance record to ensure that work has been correctly billed. If all is ok, the invoice can be passed for payment. If not it should be returned to the supplier for amendment.

A surprisingly high percentage of invoices received by contract hire companies are rejected because they do not reflect the work that was authorised.

Written maintenance policy

A written maintenance policy is a simple set of rules issued to each driver, setting out the steps they should take if work needs to be done to their car. If the car is supplied on contract hire or is professionally fleet managed, the supplier will include this information in the handbook supplied with the car.

In the absence of such an arrangement you can produce a similar document and issue it with the car.

Pre-agreed pricing

Pre-agreed pricing can considerably reduce your service, maintenance and repair costs. Discounts are available in most areas of SMR but these should be pre-agreed to maximise the discount you obtain.

Some servicing items are offered at an all-in list price ('**menu pricing**'). Here you will need to agree a flat discount off a published menu price.

Other items, such as repair work, are quoted on a '**parts plus labour**' basis. It should go without saying but you may get a great discount off the parts list price and the labour rate but unless you know how long a piece of work should take you will not be controlling your costs effectively.

If you have a pre-agreed deal with a garage they may provide courtesy cars when your cars are off the road.

OUTSOURCING MAINTENANCE

One way to avoid almost every aspect of maintenance control is to obtain your vehicles on maintenance-inclusive contract hire or use a fleet management service. Contract hire and fleet management companies employ teams of qualified maintenance controllers to carry out pre- and post-event control. These are generally time-served motor engineers who once worked at motor dealerships, carrying out the repair work they are now authorising.

They know how long each piece of work should take and can muster real buying power. As competition in the contract hire market is stiff, all the discounts they get are likely to be passed back to you in a competitive rental.

Most contract hire companies will carry out only essential safety-related work in the last few months of the contract. This is good fleet management practice for all fleets; otherwise you are wasting money.

FAST-FITS

These are the retail workshops that specialise in fitting tyres, brakes, batteries, exhausts and shock absorbers. Many lessors and fleet management companies like fast-fits because prices tend to be lower than conventional garages for this sort of repair.

Fast-fits carry huge stocks and the work can often be done by a mobile unit at the driver's office or home.

TYRES

We all want our tyres to have the highest level of grip, tread life, durability and comfort, on the motorway and minor roads, in summer and winter. And we don't want to pay too much for them either.

Sadly we cannot have all of these attributes in one tyre. Tyres represent a compromise and manufacturers have to trade off one attribute against another.

You car's manufacturer selected the tyres in consultation with the tyre manufacturer and chose the best option for the weight, style and power of the vehicle. Bear this in mind when replacing tyres. It is best to replace a worn tyre with the one the manufacturer specified, even if it costs more. You get what you pay for with tyres.

TYRE SAFETY AND THE LAW

The minimum legal tread depth for cars and similar vehicles throughout the EU is 1.6mm across a continuous band comprising the central 75% of the tread and circumference of the tyre. There must be no tears, deep cuts, lumps, bulges or separation of the components of the tyre, and no part of the underlying cords or ply should be visible.

Most car tyres have tread wear indicators – small ribs set at 1.6mm that can be found across the bottom of the main tread grooves.

For safety reasons many fleets replace their tyres at 2mm. Temporary-use '**run-flat**' tyres must not be driven faster than 50mph and must be a different colour to normal tyres.

Surveys have consistently shown that a high proportion of cars are driven with dangerously worn tyre tread.

The law on driving with defective tyres is quite harsh. For all vehicles (other than goods vehicles and vehicles adapted to carry more than eight passengers) every offence carries a fine at level 4 of the standard scale (currently £2,500) with discretionary disqualification and three penalty points. Each faulty tyre is considered a separate offence, so four faulty tyres can involve a fine of up to £10,000.

It is illegal in the UK to mix radial ply and cross ply tyres on the same axle or to have radial ply tyres on the front axle and cross ply tyres on the rear axle, except when a spare tyre is used in an emergency.

CHECKING TYRES

All tyres wear down through normal use but some wear is not mileage-related.

Wear around the inner or outer edge can be caused by poor wheel alignment or suspension problems. Bad alignment increases the speed of wear and leads to poor handling and vehicle vibration.

Tyres should always be inflated according to the manufacturer's recommendation and only when cold as the pressure rises when they are hot. Under- or over-inflation affects handling, steering and braking.

All tyres have a series of codes on their sidewall, showing the maximum weight the tyre can carry, maximum speed, country of origin, size, type approval, etc. For more information on these markings see the leaflet *Know Your Tyres* available from the **Tyre Industry Council (TIC)**. www.tyresafety.co.uk.

RETREADS AND USED TYRES

In normal use the tread is the only part of a tyre to wear away. The TIC argues it makes economic and ecological sense to give a new lease of life to an otherwise good tyre by retreading it. All retreads produced in the UK must comply with BS AU 144e, the British Standard for retreaded tyres, and must be marked with the Standard number.

Retreaded tyres are used extensively on aircraft and in motor racing. Tyre debris at the side of motorways does not necessarily come from retreaded tyres.

Are you thinking of buying part-worn or 'second-hand' tyres to save money? Bear in mind they may come from a vehicle involved in an accident or have been damaged by 'kerbing'. Repairs may not comply with British Standards. Part-worn tyres offered for sale have to have been properly examined internally and externally. Tread depth must be 2mm minimum across the whole breadth of tread and the tyres must be marked 'PART-WORN'.

DISPOSAL OF TYRES

When you have a new tyre fitted the supplier disposes of the old one. You don't have to worry about what they do with the old one because that's their concern, not yours. Right? No, actually, that's wrong.

The **EU Directive on Landfill** outlaws the burying of whole or shredded tyres. If your tyre supplier does not take this responsibility seriously you are responsible too. It is extremely unlikely that a large national tyre supplier will fail in its duty to dispose of tyres legally but some smaller operators may be less scrupulous. If your have any doubts you should check that your supplier is using a registered collection agent to dispose of your tyres legally.

WINDSCREENS

Poorly maintained roads, low flying birds, materials falling from lorries and a myriad of other things can cause windscreens to break.

An efficient industry has built up around the repair and replacement of windscreens. These companies hold vast stocks of replacement units and in most cases your windscreen can be professionally replaced at an address to suit you within hours of the damage occurring.

You may not need to replace a cracked windscreen. Some can be repaired. In a 290mm wide area directly in front of the driver, bound by the edge of the arc cleaned by the driver's windscreen wiper, you can repair a crack no larger than 10mm. In all other areas it is OK to repair a crack no larger than 40mm.

Windscreen repairs are cheap and may cost less than the excess on your comprehensive motor insurance policy. Some insurers will even pay for the repair without deduction of the excess, as it saves them the cost of a replacement window.

A trained technician should carry out a windscreen repair. They will remove any dirt from the crack, then create a vacuum over the damaged area and inject resin to fill the crack. The repair is then dried using ultra violet light and polished to make it invisible.

MANUFACTURERS' WARRANTIES

Most new cars come with three years' warranty; year 1 given by the manufacturer, the remainder given by the dealer. Warranties are usually limited to a maximum mileage.

The buyer of a used car enjoys the benefits of the warranty: It transfers with the car.

Warranties normally cover you for the full cost of rectifying any component failure or manufacturing faults.

Manufacturers usually warrant the body for corrosion for much longer than they warrant other parts of the vehicle, perhaps six to twelve years (though usually less on vans than on cars). This warranty normally covers perforation of the body by rust (that is, rust creating a hole) rather than just rusty body panels. If your car's bodywork is damaged and repaired, the anti-corrosion treatment must be restored or the corrosion warranty will be invalidated.

The manufacturer may provide a separate paintwork warranty, covering the new vehicle against fading, peeling, etc, for perhaps three years.

Even once the manufacturer's warranty has expired, they will usually entertain 'goodwill' claims (often called '**policy claims**'). They don't want to have disgruntled customers running to the press and complaining publicly if a major and expensive failure occurs soon after the warranty expires. Most manufacturers have a schedule showing the percentage of the rectification cost they will pay and how this reduces in the months after the warranty expires.

Many manufacturers now offer an extended warranty. For an additional premium they cover the vehicle for four or five years and perhaps 120,000 miles. Whether this cover is worthwhile depends on the cost and your attitude to risk.

Fuel management

How can you ensure you pay the lowest price possible, minimise fuel consumption and only pay for fuel used for authorised purposes? This is quite a tall order. Fortunately, tools exist to help you.

Fuel cards

Cost control is only achievable if you have information. Unfortunately, for many companies, fuel information is only available through analysing scraps of paper (petrol bills) and trying to make sense of what they say – a thankless task. The first step to getting control of fuel expenditure is to use a fuel card. These are used much like credit cards. The driver presents the card at the petrol station and the cashier swipes it through a reader.

Fuel cards can be configured for use by a named driver and/or a specific car, to cover petrol only or petrol and oil. You can stipulate whether vehicle mileage has to be entered at the point of sale.

You will receive one invoice (usually weekly, fortnightly or monthly) showing all fuel expenditure.

Additional reports are available – often online – and it is through these that you take control of your fuel costs. Reports can show, by driver or by car:

- The price paid per gallon/litre – allowing you to target those drivers who are spending more than they need
- The current mileage of each car – allowing you to ensure that cars are serviced at the correct time/mileage
- Mileage per gallon/litre for each vehicle – so you can spot drivers who are heavy on the accelerator pedal
- Exception reporting – showing where fuel consumption is varying from the norm
- Suspect transactions reporting – highlighting missing, dubious or inaccurate information

Fuel cards are an efficient way to collect all fuel expenses onto one invoice. They are also a form of credit – there is no need to give cash advances to staff to cover fuel costs and no need for them to use up their personal credit card limits on company fuel.

Fuel cards work well when the company is paying for all of the driver's fuel, both business and private. However, many companies have stopped providing free private fuel because the tax payable by most drivers exceeds the benefit of the free fuel. This has made many businesses think again about providing fuel cards. They have had to choose between either:

(a) Continuing to provide fuel cards and requiring the driver to submit a form analysing mileage between business and personal use; or

(b) Discontinuing the use of fuel cards completely and requiring the driver to claim for business mileage driven.

The general view in the fleet industry is that fuel cards provide such a valuable management tool that they should be retained. The company pays for all fuel used then deducts an amount from the employee's net salary for the cost of any private fuel. Employees sign a form authorising this deduction.

Fuel cards cost little or nothing. The fuel card companies pay less than the pump price so they can afford to give free fuel cards to their larger clients. If you have a big fleet they may offer you a discount off the pump price too. It may be only a fraction of a penny per litre but if you buy a lot of fuel this can add up to a tidy sum every year.

There are few fuel card operators in the UK compared with, for example, the United States, where you can choose from dozens of suppliers. If you want a card that can also be used on the Continent there are fewer still. So while in theory you can shop around, in practice you will be surprised how short your short-list will be.

Fuel cards are good but not perfect. If you want to ensure that your fuel is only going into your employee's company car, not their spouse's car, you can have their company car registration number embossed on the card. Some garages check the number but many do not. In fact, it is doubtful whether the cashier at a large motorway filling station could see the licence plate even if they tried. The cards can be configured so that mileage is captured at the point of sale but if the driver doesn't provide mileage the cashiers know they can just key zero into the mileage field to complete the transaction.

Notwithstanding their limitations, fuel cards are a valuable addition to the fleet manager's toolbox.

BUNKERING

When you buy fuel from a garage you are paying for the fuel, the garage's overheads, their profit margin and a contribution towards the losses they make when motorists drive off without paying.

Bunkering means having bulk fuel for your company vehicles delivered to your own storage facility. Once you have made the initial capital investment you pay for the fuel at wholesale prices, cutting out the garage costs.

Would bunkering make sense for your business? It works best for organisations that have a large number of vehicles working in a small geographic area, particularly vehicles that return to base every day, eg delivery vans. The tank has to be located carefully and you must comply with strict safety rules.

REPLACEMENT VEHICLE

A replacement vehicle is often offered as part of a contract hire deal. You can view this as a form of insurance. If your car is off the road because of an accident or for repair, the contract hire company will supply a temporary replacement.

Various options are available. The contract will say the replacement vehicle will be provided after your car has been off the road for 24, 48 or 72 hours, in the event of an accident or repairs or both, with a time limit of 21, 30 or 45 days.

A replacement vehicle is paid for as part of the rental, whether you use it or not. Some fleets consider this to be valuable insurance against unexpected events, while others prefer to pay for daily hire cars as required (therefore self-insuring this risk). Before including a replacement vehicle in your agreement you should weigh up the likely costs and benefits.

ROADSIDE ASSISTANCE

UK BREAKDOWN RECOVERY

Roadside assistance organisations will attend when your vehicle breaks down and either get the vehicle started or tow it to a garage. The service can be extended to cover breakdowns outside your home, transportation of the car and its occupants to the intended destination and hotel expenses.

Several players now compete in this market and this has created more price competition.

As breakdowns are unpredictable you can view a roadside assistance service as a form of insurance. And, as with most insurances, you can either buy the insurance or self-insure. Many fleets adopt a hybrid approach; paying a small annual fee per vehicle and a second charge if they actually use the service.

Manufacturers often give away 12 months' free membership of a roadside recovery organisation when you buy a new car. If you already have a fleet breakdown recovery deal, remember to take this free membership into account so you do not pay twice.

INTERNATIONAL BREAKDOWN RECOVERY

A vehicle breakdown in this country is inconvenient but a breakdown on the Continent would leave many fleet drivers wondering what to do.

International assistance gives them great peace of mind, and most roadside assistance companies offer this cover. Services can include payment for minor repairs, finding and collecting spare parts, emergency car hire, paying for alternative travel arrangements and a telephone help-line manned by English-speaking staff.

It is worthwhile including repatriation of the vehicle in the cover. Otherwise, in an extreme case, the driver could have to wait around for some days until the car is repaired, or, even worse, return home while it is being repaired and then have to return to the Continent to pick it up.

International breakdown recovery cover is usually bought by the trip, for a given number of days and people, though some suppliers also offer annual cover.

DAILY HIRE

Daily hire (vehicle rental) is a useful and cost-effective way to buy short-term mobility for your staff. You get the vehicle when you need it and someone else has to worry about depreciation, road tax, maintenance and disposal.

It may be a cheaper option than allowing your employees to use their own cars and claim mileage reimbursement. It may be safer, too, because cars hired from recognised companies are likely to be well maintained, which may not always be true of your employees' cars.

The market is very competitive. By shopping around you should get a good deal, with good volume discounts if you are likely to be a big user.

With so much choice around, how do you choose the right supplier? As with all services, it's best not to choose solely on the basis of price. If you are going to rent a lot of vehicles, consider the quality of the supplier's administration, the range of cars offered and the availability of one-way rentals.

Should you use a local company or one of the national networks? The big names in car rental appear to be everywhere and you would be forgiven for thinking they make up the whole market. In fact there are hundreds of small independent suppliers that can often offer a friendly, local, tailor-made service that you might value more than a big brand name.

A car rented from a reputable company will have been properly serviced and will be roadworthy but might not be in perfect condition. Any bodywork damage will be marked on the condition report when you take delivery of the car. The driver should always check the car and the condition report on delivery to avoid problems later.

You should also check that the driver is insured to drive the vehicle, either on your motor insurance or insurance bought from the daily hire company.

Most rental companies deliver a car with a full tank of petrol and expect you to return it with a full tank. If it is not full they will charge to fill it up, usually at a price significantly in excess of normal pump prices.

If you need a new vehicle for your fleet you can take it on a test drive or borrow a manufacturer's demonstrator vehicle. However, why not rent one for a month instead? This will give you a much better chance to check out the vehicle in real life situations. It will not cost that much and could help avoid an expensive mistake.

SPEEDING FINES AND TRAFFIC LIGHT OFFENCES

Every year around 1.5 million motorists are prosecuted for offences that are recorded on speed or traffic light cameras. The proliferation of cameras across the country has reduced the number of accidents on the roads; 100 lives a year according to the Department of Transport.

Within a few days of your car being photographed you will receive a Notice of Intended Prosecution asking for details of the driver. You must provide these details if you know who was driving. (The Privy Council has decided there is no breach of your human rights in requiring you to divulge this information. If you refuse to name the driver, your company may be prosecuted.)

Normally you will complete and return the form and in due course the driver will receive a Notice of Intended Prosecution and be prosecuted.

If your cars are leased or on contract hire, the registered keeper will receive the Notice of Intended Prosecution and advise the authorities that the vehicle is leased to you.

BUS LANE OFFENCES

Drivers can be prosecuted for driving in bus lanes without authority and many buses now carry on-board video cameras to catch bus lane offenders.

If you lease a car that is involved in a bus lane offence, the contract hire company will normally pay the fine (usually £40) and send you a recharge invoice, possibly adding an administration charge.

By paying promptly they will have saved you £40 because the charge automatically doubles to £80 if payment is delayed. However you will not have had the opportunity to challenge the validity of the fine before it has been paid. Nonetheless, you can do this subsequently should you wish.

Once convicted of a motoring offence a driver's licence is endorsed with details of the offence. Each conviction carries a number of points, depending on the seriousness of the offence. Once twelve points have been accumulated, the driver is usually automatically banned from driving for a set period of time. This is the '**totting-up**' scheme.

Each offence is given a code and these are listed in the Convictions and Endorsements section of www.direct.gov.uk. This list will help you determine conviction histories when you inspect your drivers' licences.

Penalty points count towards the totting-up scheme for three years but may remain printed on a licence for longer. For example, a dangerous driving conviction will remain on the licence for four years and a drink driving conviction remains for eleven years.

With so many speeding cameras on our roads, many drivers are being disqualified from driving under the totting-up scheme. So there is more risk that some of your drivers may be driving while disqualified: this invalidates their motor insurance.

ANNOYANCE FINES

The Police Reform Act 2002 gives police the power to issue a fixed penalty notice if vehicles are being driven in a way that might cause alarm, distress or annoyance. If the fines are not paid the police have the right to enter premises and impound vehicles.

DRINK DRIVING

Many of the 80,000 or so drivers prosecuted annually for drink-driving offences are company car drivers, and many are driving for work when caught.

You need a policy setting out what will happen if one of your drivers is banned from driving. This should deal with disciplinary sanctions (perhaps loss of benefits, withdrawal of car, dismissal, etc), what happens if they cannot do their job without being able to drive, whether they can retain the car for use by their spouse/partner, whether they should be compensated for the loss of the car (a contentious point!) and whether any cash allowance should continue to be paid.

If you publish a well thought-out and fair policy your drivers will not be able to say they did not know what would happen, and you will not have to negotiate with individual drivers once they have been caught drink-driving.

Parking fines

It's quite simple really: You park illegally, the local authority pops a ticket on your windscreen and you pay it. In most cases, if you don't pay within a certain period or if they have to send you more than one reminder, the fine increases.

Your company car policy should state clearly that it is the employee's responsibility to pay any parking fines.

If you lease your vehicles the parking fine notice will be sent to the registered keeper, normally the contract hire company, and they will forward it to you for payment. You will then normally pass the notice to the driver to pay. So some time may elapse between the notice getting from the contract hire company to the driver and there is a risk the fine will increase in the interim. Therefore a guilty driver should pay a fine as soon as the ticket has been placed on their windscreen rather than waiting for the bill to arrive.

Disposal

If you lease your vehicles or have a fleet management arrangement, the supplier will dispose of your vehicles. Otherwise you will have direct exposure to the used car market. As with most markets, the more you understand how it works, the better the price you will achieve.

Used car prices fluctuate according to a variety of macro and microeconomic factors.

If the economy is doing badly, interest rates are high, jobs are not secure and people have less money to spend, used car prices will be relatively low. When the reverse applies used car prices will be higher.

If there is low supply of used cars into the market, prices tend to rise, and vice versa if supply is high. So if you know that new cars sales reached record levels a few years ago you know that record levels of used cars will be hitting the used car market around now. If this is causing prices to fall you might wish extend your vehicle retention period to see if prices harden.

When you are deciding what cars to put on your fleet, think about the typical used car buyer. They are operating on a budget. They can't afford a new car. They have the same personal, status, fashion, practical and transport needs as buyers of new cars – they just have less to spend. They buy smaller cars because they are cheap to run, or they buy people carriers (MPVs) for family practicality. So if you are selling a lot of large executive models you do not have the cars the average buyer wants to buy and this will be reflected in the prices you achieve.

Most business cars enter the used car market after three or four years. The market price reflects how many years have elapsed since the model was introduced, ie how far it is through its life cycle. Most used cars sell for a premium for the first year after the model is introduced. Prices then flatten out for a few years and then, towards the end of the model's life cycle, they begin to decline.

There is evidence this pattern can be predicted, manufacturer-by-manufacturer. That is, each manufacturer's models tend to follow the same pattern whereby they achieve a premium price, then have a stable price and finally a declining price.

'Special editions', often launched by manufacturers to boost the sale of unpopular models nearing their replacement date, do not command a premium on resale.

The colour of the car is important in the used car market. Used car buyers are a conservative lot and they prefer red, grey, silver, black and dark blue rather than brown or green.

Some police forces now order silver rather than white cars to make these more attractive to the used car market. White paint shows marks and looks dull after a few years: in the upper medium car sector it can reduce the sale price of a car by up to £500. In fact silver (and silver/grey) is the most fashionable car colour now across the world, not just in the UK. Will it become less fashionable in time, leading to a glut of old-looking used silver cars and lower prices? Probably.

Metallic paint always scores better than non-metallic but not on vans.

Colours that sell well on small cars do not necessarily sell well on bigger cars. So, for example, a 'flat' (non-metallic) blue will be shunned on a big car but if it is quite a bright blue it will sell well on a smaller car.

Generally speaking, the larger the car the more conservative the colour should be. A poor colour can knock 10% off the sale price. Unpopular colours seem to find their way into rental fleets, then rapidly into the used car market, so prices fall.

Used car buyers like air-conditioning, electric windows and central locking. If accessories have been removed leaving holes, or if tow bars have been fitted, the value will be marked down.

Used car prices generally fall in the month before the registration plate changes in March and September. Dealers do not want to hold stocks of cars over the change date only to find these cars then look older to the buying public.

If you take delivery of a new car in February or August you will be trying to sell it three years later in a quiet used car market. If you want to lease a vehicle toward the end of those months you may well find your contract hire company asks you to wait a couple of weeks or charges a small premium for earlier delivery.

There are many ways to sell used vehicles. Generally, the closer you can get to the retail buyer the higher the price achieved, but selling to the retail buyer is also the slowest route and has most risk attached.

If you are about to de-fleet a vehicle and want to sell it promptly in the retail market, it's a good idea to advertise it as early as possible, ideally before it becomes available (though it may be difficult to arrange a test-drive if your driver still needs it for work).

If you sell a car without a V5C the dealer will apply for a new one. This takes about six weeks because the DVLA has to check the car has not been stolen. During this time the car will depreciate further and the dealer will have to pay for storage and other holding costs. Therefore dealers pay less for cars without a V5C so you should always make sure this form is available when you sell a car.

AUCTIONS

Auctions are an efficient way to sell your vehicles, achieving the fastest sale at the lowest risk.

It is generally believed that your risk ends when the hammer falls but that will depend on the selling description you have chosen.

Different auction houses adopt different selling descriptions; British Car Auctions (BCA – the largest auction group) uses the following terms:

1. No major mechanical faults – vehicles sold under this description should have no major engine, gearbox, clutch, brake or transmission faults

2. Specified faults – the auctioneer will announce the vehicle's defects

3. Sold as seen – sold as they are, with no warranties by the seller

4. On an engineer's report – with the benefit of a BCA engineer's report

If the vehicle is sold with No Major Mechanical Faults or Specified Faults, the buyer has one hour after the auction to complain to the BCA Branch Engineer about any defects not already disclosed by the seller. The Branch Engineer will investigate and if the complaint is justified the seller will be contacted to negotiate an adjustment to the price to cover the cost of rectifying the fault. If the complaint is extremely serious, the Branch Engineer will cancel the sale.

Selling a car at auction generally achieves the lowest prices because most attendees are traders buying for resale and they have to leave enough scope to achieve their profit on resale.

The auction house will advise you on valuation and setting a reserve price. Most offer a collection, valeting and refurbishment service.

It is worthwhile attending the auction. This gives you the chance to see the condition of your vehicles and helps you set accurate reserve prices. You can then amend the reserve according to how the bidding is going on the day, and if the car fails to attract the reserve price you can still do a deal there and then with the next-highest bidder.

The auction house will also advise which auction is likely to get the best price. They hold special sales targeted at different buyers and you want to sell your cars when the right type of buyer is in the auction hall.

DEALER SALE

For some years franchised dealers have faced price pressure: They get low margins on new vehicle sales and leasing companies tightly control their charges for maintenance work. So for many dealers, used car sales are one of the most profitable parts of their business. They need a ready supply of good quality stock to feed this business, and many will be happy to retail your vehicles.

Various arrangements can be made: They may simply buy your cars from you, take them on '**sale or return**' or sell them for a share of the sales proceeds.

One approach is to agree they will display your vehicles for a fixed period of, say, 40 days. If they sell during this period they will pay you, say, 90% of the sale proceeds. Otherwise they will pay you CAP or Glass's Retail price less 12%. Alternatively you might agree they will retain 100% of any proceeds over a pre-agreed figure. These arrangements give them the incentive to sell the car quickly and at the best possible price.

If you arrange for a dealer to sell your vehicles you should agree the deal in writing at the outset. Bear in mind that if the dealer sells as your agent, you will be responsible to the buyer if anything goes wrong with the vehicle. If he sells as principal he keeps this risk.

PART-EXCHANGE

Part-exchange is an efficient way to dispose of a vehicle. You agree a purchase price for the new car and a sale price for the old one, pay over the difference and enjoy **key-for-key** exchange on delivery.

Part-exchange is a good way to dispose of 'difficult' cars – damaged, old models, the wrong colour etc. A dealer will take your car because he wants to sell you a new one.

When part exchanging, consider the purchase price and the sale price separately and satisfy yourself that both are fair. An unscrupulous dealer might boost the used car price to satisfy your ego – your desire to get a great price for your car – and then give you a lower discount on the new car than you could get elsewhere.

DEALER BUY-BACK

Occasionally, as part of the negotiation for the sale of a new car, you might be able to induce the dealer to offer to buy the car back at a future date.

The buyback agreement will set out the price, date and mileage. Make sure it also says what will happen if this is not the car's actual mileage when you deliver it to the dealer, or if its condition is poor.

DEALER SALES AGENCY

Here you buy a new car, agree to appoint the dealer as your sales agent and let him have any profits above a pre-determined amount. Once again you should ensure the agreement is crystal clear about what happens if the vehicle is returned early or late, with higher or lower mileage than planned or in below average condition.

DRIVER SALE

By selling the car to the driver you can achieve a rapid sale at a price that is attractive to both parties. After all, the driver knows the car better than anyone else and has an incentive to look after it if it could be theirs one day. You will achieve a rapid sale with no disposal costs and can sell it for between trade and retail price, so both parties win.

When selling to an individual you have to give a warranty under supply of goods legislation. You can protect yourself by buying mechanical breakdown insurance and giving this to the driver with the car.

You are also legally required to ensure the vehicle is roadworthy, and that the brakes, steering, lights and tyres are in a legal condition. Otherwise you can be fined up to £5,000.

As an alternative to selling the car to the driver you could sell it to another employee or to a member their family.

In some companies, employees have made a part-time business from buying company vehicles and selling them commercially. This is not only distracting from the work they should be doing; it becomes somewhat distasteful for you and other employees to see a commercial operation being carried out on ex-company assets. To avoid this, you can set up rules limiting the number of vehicles any employee can 'deal' in during any given period.

In general, contract hire companies will only pay for safety-related or legally-required work in the last three months of a contract. This is a good policy you could adopt on all your company cars, so as to avoid unnecessary costs and pre-conditioning (*page 52*) – the tendency for company cars to need extra work, new tyres, etc, in the few months before being bought by the driver.

RETAIL SALE

If you have a very big fleet you could set up a retail site to sell your used vehicles. To many fleets, this is the Holy Grail; selling to a retail customer where you get the highest price possible. There are no dealers, traders or auction houses in the middle taking a profit.

The main downside, of course, is the cost of setting up and maintaining the site. Having a site in a prime position will generate the highest turnover but will be very expensive. Then there are the costs associated with moving vehicles to the site and preparing them for sale. The costs of marketing the vehicles – encouraging buyers to visit your site rather than going elsewhere – will also be considerable.

Some of these costs can be offset by selling add-on products at the point of sale, such as motor finance, insurance, extended warranties and so on. The retail site becomes a business in its own right, with its own risks, rewards and regulations, requiring specialist knowledge.

Whilst most large fleets steer away from this option as it is 'non-core', it could be a real option for some.

Unfortunately, retail sale is the slowest method of sale. A car can sit on a retail site for weeks and there is no guarantee it will ever sell. And while mechanical breakdown insurance is a good sales tool and may help you avoid some costs if a vehicle breaks down after you have sold it, you still have to give a Sale of Goods Act warranty to a retail buyer regarding the merchantability, fitness for purpose and description of the vehicle.

Your risk remains quite high – you are still responsible if the car explodes when the customer drives it away.

INTERNET

The internet offers an interesting route for the sale of used vehicles and without doubt it will grow into a major disposal route for corporate fleets.

There are several organisations that can advertise used vehicles for you on the internet, for a small fee.

Geography is a limiting factor. If you have a potential buyer in Scotland but you are based in London you cannot afford to drive the vehicle up there in the hope they will buy it.

PREPARATION PRIOR TO DISPOSAL

A well-presented car will achieve a sale price significantly higher than one that is poorly presented. A modest amount of money spent on preparation is almost always repaid by an increased sale price. Yet many fleets do not bother to prepare their cars prior to sale. Even a car in awful condition will benefit from a wash and vacuum. You may think the car is terrible but someone will buy it, so it pays to present it well.

'Smart repairs' are cheap and effective if the original paintwork is unbroken. Skilled technicians gently manipulate body panels back to their original shape.

You should only embark on expensive bodywork repairs after carefully considering the likely return on your investment.

Broken glass will reduce a car's price by perhaps £100. If you can get it repaired for less it may be worthwhile doing so.

If you use an auction, they should be able to prepare the vehicle for sale for you.

MANAGE RESIDUAL VALUE AND MAINTENANCE RISKS

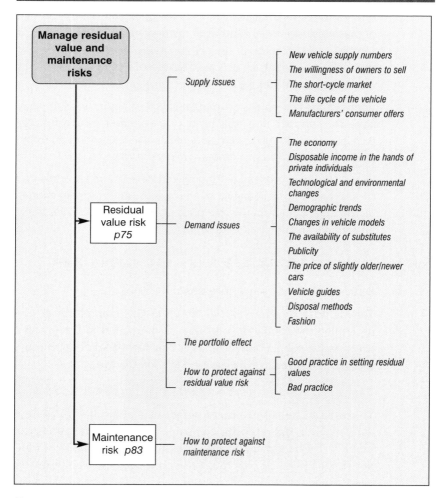

Manage residual value and maintenance risks

Supply issues
- New vehicle supply numbers
- The willingness of owners to sell
- The short-cycle market
- The life cycle of the vehicle
- Manufacturers' consumer offers

Residual value risk *p75*

Demand issues
- The economy
- Disposable income in the hands of private individuals
- Technological and environmental changes
- Demographic trends
- Changes in vehicle models
- The availability of substitutes
- Publicity
- The price of slightly older/newer cars
- Vehicle guides
- Disposal methods
- Fashion

The portfolio effect

How to protect against residual value risk
- Good practice in setting residual values
- Bad practice

Maintenance risk *p83*
- How to protect against maintenance risk

RESIDUAL VALUE RISK

Residual value (RV) risk is the risk in the price that a vehicle will achieve on resale. If you buy your own vehicles then sell them on your own account, you are taking residual value risk.

In the Disposal section (*page 66*), we looked at ways to maximise sale proceeds when you dispose of your vehicles. In this chapter we look at the decisions you will make before you acquire your vehicles, in order to reduce your risk.

A quick definition: Residual value is the price you achieve on sale of the vehicle whereas **estimated residual value** is an estimate of the likely sale proceeds of the vehicle, made when the vehicle was new. When 'residual value' is used to describe both situations this can lead to confusion.

Contract hire companies estimate residual values for a living. They have to: contract hire, the product demanded most often by British businesses, gives complete residual value protection to the client. The contract hire company takes this risk.

In assessing this risk and setting an estimated residual value, you should take into account all of the macro- and micro-economic factors that can affect the sale price of a car. We can divide these into supply and demand issues.

Supply issues to consider when estimating RVs

New vehicle supply numbers

The number of new vehicles entering the market today will determine the supply of used cars in the market in three years' time. As the supply of new vehicles was high from 2005 to 2007, the supply of used cars will be high in 2008 to 2010.

The willingness of owners to sell their cars

This used to be easy to measure because about half of all new vehicles were operated by companies and sold after thirty-six months. This is now slightly less certain as many companies are now running vehicles for four years to reduce average costs. 20 years ago many companies kept vehicles for just two years.

Private owners are also extending ownership cycles and more will do so if the economy cools.

The short-cycle market

Manufacturers supply heavily-discounted new vehicles to daily hire companies and large fleets. The number of vehicles currently entering the short-cycle market has a direct impact on the number of nearly-new cars hitting the used car market in a year's time. If this is a large number it will have a knock-on effect on the price of used cars in two or three years' time.

In estimating residual values you need to consider the likelihood of such deals continuing.

THE LIFE CYCLE OF THE VEHICLE

You need to consider whether a vehicle will still be a current model at the time of sale.

MANUFACTURERS' CONSUMER OFFERS

Manufacturers often use special offers to promote particular models, normally targeting retail rather than fleet buyers. You should be aware of these deals as they depress the new price of a vehicle and therefore have a direct effect on the used price.

DEMAND ISSUES TO CONSIDER WHEN ESTIMATING RVS

THE ECONOMY

You will have to consider the general economic climate (gross domestic product, inflation, interest rates, employment, etc) and the amount of disposable income in the hands of private individuals.

Private individuals buy the vast majority of used cars. Although more companies have bought used cars in the last few years, this is still not the norm. Where companies do buy used cars, most of these cars are less than twelve months old and the supply of these varies according to how many cars the manufacturers feed into the daily hire market.

Disposable income is a function of economic growth, employment, interest rates and the willingness of people to part with their savings.

TECHNOLOGICAL AND ENVIRONMENTAL CHANGES

Three years is long enough for technology, legislation or fashion to change and affect the attractiveness of a used vehicle to a buyer. Some changes can be foreseen and you can attempt to measure their likely effect on residual values. Others are harder to measure. For example, the sharp increase in the number of company car drivers choosing diesel cars perplexed many RV-setters who had to decide how the used car market would accept a sharp increase in the number of used diesels.

DEMOGRAPHIC TRENDS

Demographic trends in the UK population are likely to make some cars more popular than others. With an ageing population, smaller cars are likely to gain in popularity over large, expensive ones.

CHANGES IN VEHICLE MODELS BY MANUFACTURERS

Old models look old and are not as attractive to the used car buyer. Product life cycles vary. By reading motoring publications you can usually ascertain whether a model change is likely to occur within the next year or two and whether it is going to be a facelift or a total replacement. However, it is not normally possible to get information on model changes planned for later than this.

THE AVAILABILITY OF SUBSTITUTES

The buyer of a three-year-old Ford Mondeo 1.8 this summer is likely to have a fixed budget. If, for reasons listed under 'supply' above, the prices of used Mondeo 1.8s are high, they will buy a different make or model and prices for those models will rise. The substitution effect is very real but is very hard to predict or measure.

PUBLICITY

Adverse publicity about a particular make or model of vehicle will affect its resale value.

For example, the old Vauxhall Senator was derided as a 'gas-guzzler' for years until a very favourable BBC Top Gear review significantly increased the used price. And Rover Group's well-publicised problems did nothing to help the used prices of Rover and MG vehicles.

Positive publicity tends to lift prices. The latest generation of

Skoda cars has impressed the pundits and clever tongue-in-cheek advertising has helped reposition the brand, leading to much better residual values.

THE PRICE OF SLIGHTLY OLDER/NEWER CARS

The prices of 12, 18 and 24 month old cars are strongly affected by manufacturers' efforts to maintain output and market share. As already discussed, they offer large discounts to daily rental and other companies who buy cars in bulk and dispose of them within 12 months. These deals distort the market for nearly new cars and this has a direct 'knock-on' effect on the prices of older cars of the same model.

VEHICLE GUIDES

Having already said that current values are used as a starting place for future value projections, and given the fact that traders use published guides to determine the current market price of a used vehicle, it is obvious that the published guides are an important factor in this market.

Glass's Guide and CAP Black Book are monthly publications that take data from auctions and calculate average market values. Parker's Guide is available to consumers at stationers.

Every now and then one of these guides may report that, in its opinion, a certain vehicle is under- or over-valued. The trade responds accordingly.

DISPOSAL METHODS

The price achieved in a private sale is usually significantly higher than the price achieved at auction.

FASHION

Some vehicle colours enhance sale values while others tend to devalue a vehicle (*see page 67*). The used vehicle market has come to expect that some optional extras will be fitted to certain vehicles, and prices will be marked down if these extras are missing.

THE PORTFOLIO EFFECT

If you have a large mixed fleet you will be cushioned against some market downturns by the portfolio effect – an over-estimation on one vehicle may be compensated for by an under-estimation on another.

Contract hire companies routinely get their sums wrong when estimating residual values on individual cars but the portfolio effect helps them. Generally they gain if the used car market rises unexpectedly and they lose if it falls unexpectedly.

The volatility of the used car market can be shown from this chart, showing the movement in year-on-year prices across a range of fleet cars since 2000:

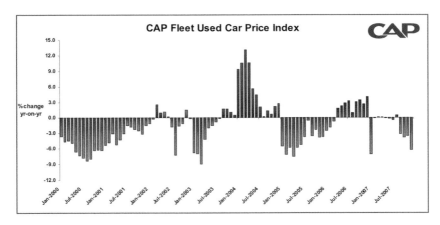

Source: CAP Motor Research

HOW TO PROTECT AGAINST RESIDUAL VALUE RISK

If you acquire vehicles using a finance lease or a 'purchase' acquisition method you are fully exposed to residual value risk.

If you estimate that the residual value of a vehicle will be £5,000 and it sells for only £4,000, the loss (the extra depreciation) is all yours. You can shift this risk to another party by entering into a buy-back agreement with the dealer that supplied the car, or by funding your vehicles on contract hire, operating lease, daily hire or contract purchase.

Like all forecasting, estimating residual values is part art, part science. And getting it wrong can be expensive.

If you take your own residual value risk and need help setting residuals, there are several publications on the market that can help you. None is likely to be more reliable than the others and their historical accuracy is no guarantee of future performance.

You can buy insurance to cover residual value risk. If your want to remove the full residual risk, you will find this cover is hard to obtain and is very expensive as you will be giving the insurer the full risk without giving them control of the vehicle maintenance or disposal, the two key tools to reduce RV risk.

However, if you just want to remove vehicles from your balance sheet, the cover should be easier to obtain and less expensive, as the insurer should be able to remove some of your risk (enough to make your accountants happy) while keeping their risk manageable.

GOOD PRACTICE IN SETTING RESIDUAL VALUES

If you are taking your own residual value risk you need to estimate your own residual values. Otherwise you will be unable to determine whole-life costs and unable to decide which vehicles to put on your fleet.

This checklist sets out good and bad practice in estimating residual values.

When estimating residual values

Good practice:

- Follow macro-economic developments and have an agreed company position on the likely strength of the UK economy and consumer confidence in two, three and four years' time.
- Obtain information about vehicle supply numbers for each make/model.
- Decide how likely it is that the owners of a particular make and model of vehicle will dispose of them in two, three and four years' time.

- Consider all of the technological, environmental and fashion issues likely to affect used car values.
- Monitor upcoming changes in vehicle models.
- Consider how attractive a particular vehicle will be to a used car buyer, compared with other similar vehicles in its class.
- Monitor manufacturers' marketing activities, particularly heavy discounts to daily rental companies and rapid cycle schemes and consider how these are likely to affect used car prices.
- Consider whether your disposal method is consistently likely to produce CAP Average, CAP Clean or some other benchmark sale price. If you consistently get 5% above CAP Clean you can reflect this in your estimated residual values.
- Subscribe to a publication such as CAP Monitor that predicts residual values, though don't follow it blindly.
- Arrange alternative disposal routes for individual vehicles if you face a large residual value loss. For example, market these vehicles strongly to your staff and their families.
- Consider adjusting estimated residual values to reflect vehicle colours and optional extras.
- Review estimated residual values frequently.
- Consider whether any special events will occur at the time of disposal that may affect sale patterns, for example the World Cup, Christmas or some other event that will distract buyer attention.
- Adjust estimated residual values to reflect how and where the vehicle is to be driven. (Published residual value estimates assume average driving conditions.)
- Produce reports showing how you have arrived at your residual values estimates.

Bad practice:
- Allowing any one person to dominate the residual value setting process.
- Relying too heavily on any one publication.

After sale of the vehicle

Good practice:

- Monitor sales performance against CAP Black Book. If you are consistently selling vehicles above (or below) CAP Average, take this into account when estimating residual values.

- Produce reports showing sale performance relative to CAP Average and Clean.

Maintenance risk

Vehicles are complex pieces of machinery with many components and moving parts. Like all such equipment, occasionally they go wrong. A regularly serviced vehicle is likely to need fewer expensive repairs than a vehicle where servicing has been skipped.

If you own a vehicle, are buying it using a 'purchase method' of finance or leasing it on non-maintenance contract hire, you bear all the cost of servicing, maintenance and repair. If the vehicle is expensive to service, has expensive parts or has more than its fair share of problems, you will have to bear the cost. In the industry's parlance, you are bearing the 'maintenance risk'.

How to protect against maintenance risk

If you want to take this risk you need to obtain information about the likely cost of maintenance. This information is available from a variety of independent sources or you can look at the rentals quoted by contract hire companies to see how much they are charging for maintenance.

It is surprisingly easy to quantify service and maintenance costs as they arise with known regularity and cost. Around 75% of the cost of maintaining a vehicle is made up of manufacturer-scheduled servicing, maintenance, replacement of worn parts (such as brake pads) and tyres.

The frequency of component failure is well known too, by make and model. However, models change frequently, so just as a few years' data have been accumulated and conclusions about reliability have been arrived at, the manufacturer introduces a new model and you have to start assembling data from scratch.

Instead of doing it yourself a contract hire or fleet management company can maintain your vehicles and take the maintenance risk. In exchange for a flat monthly charge, included in the contract hire rental or the fleet manager's charges, the supplier will pay for all of the service maintenance and repair work on the vehicle. If their estimates of the cost of running the vehicle prove incorrect, they take the loss (or indeed the profit). In either event, you get peace of mind from knowing that you have to pay only a fixed amount and that the risk is no longer yours.

8 UNDERSTAND YOUR HEALTH AND SAFETY OBLIGATIONS

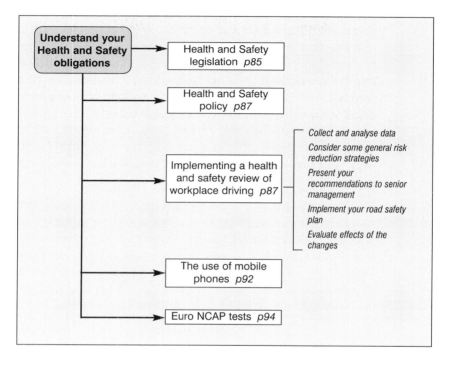

Each year in Britain more than 300,000 people are injured on the roads, 34,000 are seriously injured and 3,000 die. According to the government, 'for the majority of people, the most dangerous thing they do while at work is drive on the public highway'.

If you drive 25,000 miles each year you are as likely to die on the road as a miner in a coal mine or a construction worker on a building site.

HEALTH AND SAFETY LEGISLATION

The **Health and Safety at Work Act** gives employers a 'duty to ensure so far as is reasonably practicable the health, safety and welfare at work of all employees.' Driving 'for work' is 'at work' for this purpose and so is driving between offices or from home to a work-related course. Commuting to work in the employee's own car is not 'at work' but a detour to a client en route to work constitutes being 'at work'.

So your health and safety policy has to cover car use regardless of how you acquire your cars and even if an employee uses their own car for work. You cannot absolve your company from its health and safety responsibilities by moving from company cars to a cash-for-car or ECO scheme. In fact, many fleets that moved to cash-for-car schemes have called in health and safety consultants to look at the new risks this creates. Some have moved back to company cars, fearing they will otherwise be responsible for at-work accidents occurring in employees' cars over which they have no control.

The **Management of Health and Safety at Work Regulations** require that you assess the risks your employees are exposed to at work and examine how these can be reduced. If you have more than five employees you must keep a record of this assessment and advise employees on risks and how to reduce them. If a group of employees is at particularly high risk you must identify them and record the details.

A 'competent person' (suitably qualified) needs to assess and implement any steps that need to be taken to reduce the risks. You must plan, organise and control the risks, and face prosecution if you fail to do so, even if an accident has not occurred.

The **Health and Safety Executive (HSE)** is the government department responsible for promoting safe working practices, investigating accidents and launching safety-related prosecutions. It provides guidance on all health and safety issues, including driving-related safety issues and has a lot of material designed to help employers manage at-work motoring risks. www.hse.gov.uk

Under **The Provision and Use of Work Equipment Regulations**, equipment used at work must be suitable for the task. Legal experts believe this definition includes employee-owned vehicles used on their employer's business.

The **Work Related Road Safety Task Group (WRRTSG)** says one third of the 3000+ fatal road accidents each year in the UK are work-related. Incredibly, only 600 people die in all other work-related accidents each year.

The WRRTSG encourages fleet managers to reduce the number and length of road journeys their drivers take, plan routes in advance, reduce long hours spent driving, assess drivers' capabilities, take precautions, check drivers' licences, consider whether drivers need glasses and look at their accident histories and motoring convictions. If fleet managers are unable to assess these, they should get help.

The **Occupational Road Safety Alliance (ORSA)** is a valuable resource for employers wishing to learn more about road safety. www.orsa.org.uk

HEALTH AND SAFETY POLICY

As we have seen, there is a legal requirement for every company to assess the risks its employees are exposed to and to put in place measures to reduce these risks.

The first step for most organisations is to produce a formal Health and Safety Policy document that states the company's commitment to safety at work and the rules they expect their staff to follow. The managing director or owner should sign the policy.

IMPLEMENTING A HEALTH AND SAFETY REVIEW OF WORKPLACE DRIVING

This section sets out general guidance on assessing the risk of road accidents in your business and how you might manage those risks. This is a thumbnail sketch of a complex area and should be considered as guidance only, not definitive or prescriptive. Also, do remember that The Management of Health and Safety at Work Regulations require that a competent person must carry out your risk assessment.

These are the steps in the risk assessment.

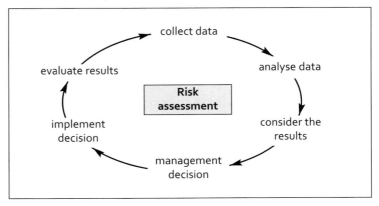

COLLECT DATA

You need to collect accident data but may be surprised at how little you have to hand.

Tucked away in files there may be details of accidents reported to your insurer but it is quite possible you will have no record at all of the minor accidents that did not lead to a claim. These accidents are important though; if several vehicles have had minor collisions when driving out of your car park, it may be time to alter the exit arrangements (layout, obstacles, signage, bushes, etc) before a more serious accident occurs.

Assemble a list of all of the accidents that have occurred in the last five years, showing:

- Name and address of the driver
- Their normal office or depot location
- Driver's age and sex
- Time of day of the accident
- How long the driver had worked for the company
- Date of their last eye test
- Information on any health problems reported
- Their manager's name
- Whether the driver was at fault
- The make, model, mileage and age of the vehicle
- Whether the vehicle servicing was up to date at the time of the accident

- Damage to own vehicle caused by the accident
- Damage to third party vehicle caused by the accident
- Location of the accident
- Distance from the driver's home and normal place of work
- Whether the driver had been speeding
- Road and weather conditions
- The type of vehicle driven by the third party
- The nature of the collision (head on, hit while parking, etc)
- The manoeuvre that your driver was doing (reversing, turning, etc)
- The manoeuvre that the other vehicle was doing (reversing, turning, etc)
- The nature of any injuries to the driver and third parties
- Any other relevant factors, eg alcohol, drugs or illness
- Any defects reported on your vehicle
- The cost of the incident
- The cause of the accident
- The action that was taken after the accident (driver training, disciplinary action, dismissal)
- Any other relevant information

ANALYSE THE DATA

Look for trends or patterns in the report. Carefully consider how to measure the data. It may be better to consider the number of accidents, write-offs, and injuries per thousand miles driven rather than just the number of accidents.

Establish the true cost to the business of road accidents. Repair and excess charges are the tip of the iceberg. The real cost includes downtime, time off work, administration and increased insurance premiums.

Look for specific areas needing attention.

For example:

- If new drivers are having accidents, do you need a better induction system for them?
- Are accidents occurring when your employees' family members are driving the company's cars? What can be done?

Train them too? Ban driving by family members below a certain age?

- Did some accidents occur when your drivers were using their mobile phones? Would a total ban on using mobile phones be practical?
- Is one manager's area having more accidents per business mile than others? Might this be evidence he is pressurising drivers to do too much in each day?
- Is there evidence that drivers are failing to take road safety seriously? If so, show them road safety videos, put safety reminder stickers in their vehicles and take other steps to remind them that safety is of paramount importance.
- Is there evidence that driver training may be necessary?
- Have there been many accidents during long journeys? If so, could you alter work rosters to remove the need for long journeys?

CONSIDER SOME GENERAL RISK REDUCTION STRATEGIES

As well as identifying the causes of past problems, these are some general steps you can consider to reduce the likelihood of accidents.

- Reduce the overall level of business driving, through videoconferencing, telephone conferencing and better planning of work journeys.
- Reduce the number of hours that can be driven in a day and the time that can be spent driving without a break.
- Use telematics to measure the hours driven and the average and maximum speed.
- Limit distances being driven in any day.
- Include safety items such as curtain airbags, anti-lock braking systems and high-visibility brake lights in all vehicles.
- Alter the colour of the vehicles being selected so that only bright colours are chosen.
- Attach reflective decals to make vehicles more visible.
- Issue your drivers with a checklist of the vehicle safety checks they should carry out every day, week and month. Mileage or expenses claims should include a certificate signed by the driver confirming they have carried out these checks.

- Only select cars that get high marks in Euro NCAP tests (*see page 94*).
- Ensure vehicles are serviced promptly. An office-based system should identify missed services and alert drivers to book in the vehicle.
- When cars are serviced or repaired, use only manufacturer-approved consumables and spare parts.
- Require drivers to notify you as soon as any fault occurs that may prejudice road safety.
- Inspect drivers' licences when they join the company or are given the right to drive company vehicles for the first time. Check these again every six months.
- Include safety packs in each car and train your drivers on how to use these.
- Ensure drivers know the loading capacity of their vehicles and instruct them never to overload a vehicle.
- Tell drivers to refuse any request from a manager to drive in a manner, or on a journey, or in a vehicle they consider unsafe or where doing so would increase the risk of an accident. Tell them to contact the health and safety officer or the fleet manager if they do not believe their manager is taking their concerns seriously.
- Require all drivers to have their eyesight tested regularly and to report the date and outcome to the company, even if they do not wear spectacles.
- Require all drivers to sign the health and safety policy annually, to reaffirm their commitment to the company's safety standards.
- Appoint a road safety improvement committee, drawn from around the business, to meet regularly, review accidents and develop improved working practices.
- Consider charging the driver if they have an accident. Many companies do this, typically charging the excess amount on the insurance policy.
- Consider an incentive scheme to reward careful driving. These have been successful but can create a culture where minor accidents are not reported.

- Employ an accident management company. They will collate information on your accidents, analyse the data and give recommendations.
- Fit speed limiters to your cars. These will give you fuel savings and reduce the severity of speed-related accidents.

PRESENT YOUR RECOMMENDATIONS TO SENIOR MANAGEMENT

Senior management need to 'buy into' the findings. Agree an action plan and specify who is responsible for implementing the recommendations. It is normal for several departments to be involved in implementing such plans.

IMPLEMENT YOUR ROAD SAFETY PLAN

Consider whether a change in your employment contracts or the company car policy would help reduce accidents. Many companies make it clear in these documents that every road accident will be investigated and they set out the consequences should the employee be at fault. Repeat 'offenders' may have their company vehicle removed. Other disciplinary measures may be taken, including dismissal.

Launch your changes with as much publicity as possible within the organisation. Issue revised driver handbooks. Get the managing director to address all drivers on the changes.

EVALUATE THE EFFECTS OF THE CHANGES

Every three months, review the changes you have made and their effectiveness. Consider whether further changes are necessary and, if so, propose these to senior management.

THE USE OF MOBILE PHONES

If you expect drivers to use mobile phones when driving for work and they then have an accident, the employer and employee may both be held responsible.

UK law bans drivers from making a call with a hand-held phone, except when calling the emergency services. See www.roads.dft.gov.uk.

The precise wording of the legislation is:

'No person shall drive a motor vehicle on a road if he or she is using a hand-held mobile telephone. A mobile telephone is to be treated as hand-held if it is, or must be, held at some point during the course of making or receiving a call.'

Drivers can still press a button to receive a call so long as the phone is not held.

This chart explains the rules.

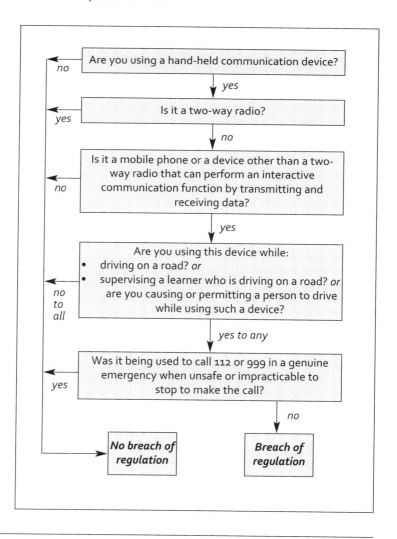

A hand-held mobile phone can be used whilst the vehicle is stationary, even if the engine is running, but not when the vehicle is at traffic lights or held up in traffic.

Employers can be prosecuted if they 'cause or permit' their employees to use a hand-held mobile phone for work when driving.

It's a good idea is set up a message that says 'I am driving and cannot take your call. Please leave a message and I will call you back when it is safe to do so'.

In 2004 a delivery driver was convicted of causing death by dangerous driving when driving for work and using a hand-held mobile phone. This breached his employer's regulations as clearly set out in the driver handbook the driver had signed. The Crown Prosecution Service said it would not prosecute the employer because it had a robust policy. The message here is clear; a well-written driver handbook reflecting best practice can save your company from prosecution.

EURO NCAP TESTS

Euro NCAP (European New Car Assessment Programme) is an independent body that tests vehicles to see how they would perform in different types of crash. It is backed by five European governments, the European Commission, many consumer organisations and motoring organisations in every European country.

Euro NCAP uses a star system to rate each vehicle it tests. Their website lists all the vehicles tested to date and shows how they have scored. www.euroncap.com.

9 GET YOUR ADMINISTRATION RIGHT

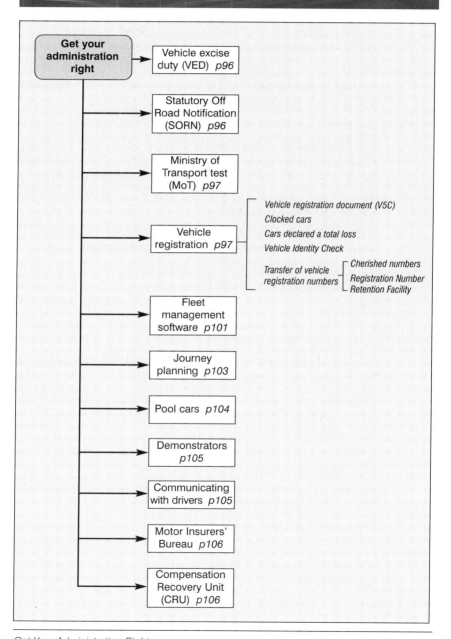

This chapter deals with issues that arise in the day-to-day running of a fleet.

VEHICLE EXCISE DUTY (VED)

VED is still commonly called road fund tax, road fund licence, car tax or the tax disc. The correct name is vehicle excise duty (VED).

The registered keeper must ensure the vehicle is continuously taxed if used or kept on a public road.

The registered keeper of the vehicle normally receives a VED renewal reminder form V11 during the month before the old tax disc expires. The form has to be taken to a post office with a valid motor insurance certificate and MoT certificate and a cheque for the amount payable. Or it can be renewed online. www.vehiclelicence.gov.uk

If your vehicles are on contract hire the supplier will send you a new tax disc about a week before the old one expires.

If you have a large fleet buying tax discs can be a chore. This task can be outsourced to a fleet management company for a small fee. They use electronic links with the DVLA to renew tax discs.

STATUTORY OFF ROAD NOTIFICATION (SORN)

If you plan to keep a vehicle off the public highway it does not need a tax disc but you must complete an official declaration (that is, you must 'declare SORN'). If you fail to do so they can fine you the higher of five times the annual rate of duty or £1,000, plus any unpaid duty, even if your vehicle is off the road. So doing nothing is no longer an option when a tax disc expires.

If you plan to keep a vehicle off the road, perhaps because the driver is working abroad, you must immediately submit a SORN. The road fund licence renewal form contains a SORN declaration notice. You can also declare SORN at www.vehiclelicence.gov.uk.

If you apply for a VED refund you can declare SORN on the refund application form V14 or V33.

It is a criminal offence to make a false SORN declaration.

MINISTRY OF TRANSPORT TEST (MOT)

By law, cars and vans are required to undergo the test at a Department of Transport-approved testing station before the third anniversary of their registration date and annually thereafter.

The test covers lighting, steering, suspension, brakes, tyres, wheels, seatbelts, exhaust system, exhaust emissions and other safety-related aspects of the vehicle but not engine, clutch or gearbox. Interestingly in these environmentally-focused days, the test measures carbon monoxide but not carbon dioxide.

If you get a new MoT certificate during the month before the old one expires, the new one will be post-dated to commence when the old one expires, so long as you produce the old certificate at the time of the test.

The rules are slightly different for a minibus or any vehicle designed to carry more than eight people. The MoT certificate contains boxes on which the test station must confirm the number of seat belts fitted and whether a seat belt test has been carried out. The old MoT certificate for a minibus always has to be handed to the MoT test station.

If you have a problem with an MoT certificate (eg you are buying a car and believe the MoT certificate is a forgery), you can get advice from www.vosa.gov.uk.

All MoT testing stations are linked by computer system. Certificates are printed out rather than handwritten and records are stored electronically, including records of vehicle mileages.

VEHICLE REGISTRATION

VEHICLE REGISTRATION DOCUMENT (V5C)

The DVLA issues this document for every vehicle sold or imported into Great Britain. It shows the registered keeper of the vehicle, who may or may not be the owner of the vehicle.

The V5C contains an extract of information held on the Register of Vehicles at the DVLA.

You must advise the DVLA if the registered keeper's name or address changes or if the vehicle is modified and its description on the V5C becomes inaccurate. For example, if you replace an engine the new engine number will not match the number on the V5C. Failure to notify the DVLA of such changes can lead to a fine. Knowingly giving false information can result in a fine and imprisonment.

If you sell a vehicle or transfer it to another person, you must notify the DVLA by following the instructions shown on the V5C. EU regulations say the V5C has to be carried in the vehicle when driving anywhere within the EU but this regulation is rarely enforced.

Other than when applying online, it is mandatory to present either a V11 reminder form or a V5C to obtain a tax disc.

CLOCKED CARS

You are encouraged but not required to enter your VAT number and the vehicle's mileage onto the V5C when selling it to a trader. This helps prevent the 'clocking' of vehicles – turning back the mileage to increase the vehicle's value.

An estimated 25% of cars are clocked at some stage and this costs consumers £150m pa. Buyers believe they are getting safe, relatively low-mileage cars but many are buying high-mileage clocked cars that may be unsafe.

It is illegal to sell a clocked car (though oddly, it is not illegal to clock one). The dealer must properly describe a vehicle, and if it is described as having a lower mileage than it has travelled, the dealer is committing an offence.

CARS DECLARED A TOTAL LOSS

If you have comprehensive motor insurance and your vehicle is written off, that's probably the last time you will think about it. The insurance company pays your claim and you concentrate on replacing the vehicle. Disposal of the vehicle is left to the insurance company.

However, if you self-insure you have to worry about vehicle disposal. There is a risk that a car declared a total loss by the insurer will be bolted back together again by a back-street repair shop then sold on to an unsuspecting member of the public. To ensure this does not happen, insurers report total loss vehicles to the DVLA and the **Motor Insurance Anti-Fraud & Theft Register (MIAFTR)**.

MIAFTR keeps a list of all vehicles that have been the subject of total loss claims, and whenever an insurer issues a new policy they check with MIAFTR to ensure the vehicle is not on the list.

If you run a big self-insured fleet and one of your vehicles is damaged beyond economic repair, you should use form V23 to advise the DVLA. If you want to be public-spirited and ensure it does not end up being put back on the road by back-street repairers, you can register details of the vehicle with MIAFTR. See www.abi.org.uk

MIAFTR defines four categories of vehicles:

A. Scrap value only. No economically salvageable parts. Only value is as scrap metal. This may be the result of the vehicle being burnt out.

B. Can be broken up for spare parts.

C. Repairable but repair costs will exceed the value of the car.

D. Other repairable vehicles, including vehicles that could have been economically repaired but the insurer chose not to do so (perhaps because it would have taken too long).

Category A and B vehicles must never be returned to the road.

If you self-insure, you must notify the DVLA on form V23 as soon as you have identified that you have a Category A, B or C vehicle.

If you are the registered keeper and an insurer makes a total loss payment to you, you must notify the DVLA (unless the insurer does so for you) by using the red section of the V5C, and then destroy the rest of the V5C.

If you self-insure and sell a Category A, B or C vehicle to a salvage company you are advised to give them a photocopy of the V5C and not the original. If anyone tries to re-register a Category A, B or C vehicle the DVLA will ask the police to investigate.

MIAFTR passes information on all total loss vehicles to the credit agencies Equifax HPI and Experian. If any future purchaser tries to buy one of these on finance, the finance company will be alerted to its 'total loss claim' history.

All Category A vehicles must be crushed. The shell, frame and chassis of Category B vehicles must be crushed as soon as any salvageable components have been removed. Category C and D vehicles can be sold on for repair.

If you self-insure and ask a salvage agent to dispose of a vehicle, you may be fined under the **Environmental Protection Act (EPA)** if the vehicle is disposed of incorrectly. You should only use a salvage agent that can guarantee it complies with the terms of the Act because the EPA obligation is yours and cannot be delegated to a third party.

VEHICLE IDENTITY CHECK

If a vehicle is written off as a total loss and is subsequently repaired, it must be inspected by the Vehicle & Operator Services Agency to confirm its identity before it can be returned to the road. The V5C will be marked to note that it has passed this test.

This is a crime-reduction measure. Each year the identities of thousands of written-off cars are transferred to stolen cars that are then sold to on to innocent buyers.

TRANSFER OF VEHICLE REGISTRATION NUMBERS

CHERISHED NUMBERS

The DVLA provides a Cherished Transfer Facility that allows a registration number to be moved directly from one vehicle to another. Both vehicles must be currently licensed, subject to annual testing and available for inspection. However, an unlicensed donor vehicle will still be considered if its licence expired no more than six months before the date of the application or if it is less than 3 years old (less than 1 year old for HGVs). Recipient vehicles must be currently licensed.

To transfer a registration number, use a V317 transfer application form, available from the DVLA.

If you wish to retain the use of a registration number but don't have a vehicle on which to use it – eg you have just sold the vehicle bearing your cherished number and have yet to replace it – you can apply to retain the number using the DVLA Retention Facility. Apply using a V778/1 retention application form, available from the DVLA.

This facility lasts 12 months and can be extended annually provided it is not allowed to lapse. Only the registered keeper of a vehicle is entitled to apply.

FLEET MANAGEMENT SOFTWARE

If you are running your own fleet of vehicles, especially if you are managing them yourself rather than using contract hire or a fleet management service, you need to keep on top of your fleet information.

You need a good diary system (to remind you when to replace vehicles and to renew vehicle excise duty, motor insurance and MoTs). You also need full service histories, fuel consumption information and so on. A good system will help you to identify abuse by drivers and garages, make it easier to make warranty claims and identify when a vehicle needs servicing.

You could keep this information in a manual filing system. Some of it is already captured in your accounting system and if your fleet is small you can probably keep a simple record card for each vehicle. However, manual systems are not ideal for collating, comparing or rapidly accessing large quantities of data, and accounting systems do not hold information in ways that are useful to a fleet manager. So at some point it will become useful for you to use specialised software to help you run the fleet.

There are several packages available, costing from a few hundred pounds – designed to help the busy manager of a small fleet to organise their day – up to hundreds of thousands of pounds for a system that will manage a large complex fleet.

Some suppliers can also provide you with useful vehicle data such as new and used vehicle prices and predicted maintenance costs.

You can find the suppliers of these systems through adverts placed in fleet publications.

When selecting fleet software these are a few things to consider:

- Decide what you need before you start talking to possible suppliers.
- Distinguish between the things you need and those that would be nice to have.
- Check their offerings against your 'needs' list.
- Make sure that there are no misunderstandings between you and the supplier as to the meaning of technical words.
- Consider sending out an invitation to tender, describing your requirements and asking them to respond point by point. Tell them the responses will form part of any contract you may subsequently sign.
- Check their references. Speak to existing clients. Are they happy?
- Check their financial clout. They may have great software but if they are unlikely to be around to support you or develop the software you would be better off looking elsewhere.
- Meet their staff. You will be relying on them, possibly for many years. How experienced are they?
- Make sure the system will cope with your growth plans.
- If you operate in several countries, consider whether you need the system to handle several currencies and, if so, make sure it can do so.
- Consider whether you like the technology they are using.

If you take your vehicles on contract hire, or engage a fleet management company, you may be able to get much of the functionality you need through online access to their systems. Do bear in mind that this is their system, not yours, so if you have several different suppliers your information will be scattered over several systems, and if you change fleet supplier you will lose access to these tools and this data.

E-COMMERCE

The next step in the development of your relationship with your contract hire or fleet management company is to use their web-based e-commerce system.

An increasing number of players in the market now offer e-commerce facilities, including quoting, management reporting, vehicle ordering and disposal, extension processing, facilities to change driver details and cost centres and more.

JOURNEY PLANNING

If you only have perk cars in your fleet you can comfortably skip this section. On the other hand, if your fleet is involved in distribution, journey planning is already a central part of your fleet management and you are likely to be an expert in the subject. Most fleets fit somewhere between these two extremes.

Mileage costs money; fuel cost, depreciation, tyres, servicing, repairs, component failure and even the number of accidents are all mileage-related. So you can reduce these costs by reducing mileage.

The easiest approach is to eliminate the need for the journey in the first place. Video-conferencing companies make their living from this idea. But if a journey has to happen, the next step is to try to minimise the number of miles that are driven. That's where journey planning comes in.

If your business has service engineers or salesmen on the road, you can plan their days to minimise mileage by devising a route that allows them to move from one call to another without zigzagging backwards and forwards around the country

There are a number of tools available to help you plan their routes. The simplest tools are websites such as maps.google.com and www.multimap.com, where you enter your start point and destination and they calculate the best route, giving step-by-step instructions and a route map.

Another approach is to use one of the many CD-based mapping systems sold in the high street or available from some motoring organisations.

The ultimate step is to put the telematics technology inside the vehicle for the driver to use. These systems start with simple sat-nav devices and at the top end can inform you and the driver about the vehicle's location, routes, speed etc, in real time or using historic information.

POOL CARS

If most of your employees only drive for work occasionally, you might like to keep a few pool cars rather than providing dedicated company cars.

As employees do not consider that the pool car is 'theirs', you will not need to buy high-specification cars; a smaller-engined vehicle – maybe even a used vehicle – that does the job and no more will often suffice.

It can however be quite difficult to manage pool cars. Demand is unlikely to be constant so they may sit idle for several days and you may then find you don't have enough of them.

The ideal approach is to have enough pool cars to ensure that they are in near-constant use and to use daily hire cars to meet any extra demand.

Another problem is that pool cars tend to be treated poorly by drivers. No one driver feels any 'ownership' of a pool car so they are unlikely to keep it clean or worry about checking oil, tyres etc.

Generally though, pool cars are a good flexible resource. They can be acquired in the same way that you acquire the remainder of your fleet; for example, outright purchase or contract hire. They do not attract benefit-in-kind tax.

In the past few years quite a lot of work has been done to introduce modern technology to the management of pool cars. Electronic boxes can be fitted that allow authorised drivers to book the vehicle electronically (via text message or over the internet), gain access by using a smart card and deactivate the immobiliser by keying in a PIN number. The vehicle keys are securely stored in the vehicle.

DEMONSTRATORS

Manufacturers know you are more likely to buy a vehicle if you are given a reasonable period in which to test-drive it, so they operate quite large fleets of demonstrator vehicles.

If your fleet is large and you have a direct relationship with a manufacturer they will supply demonstrators direct, otherwise your contract hire or fleet management company can arrange these for you.

COMMUNICATING WITH DRIVERS

There is quite a lot of information that you need to provide to, or receive from, your drivers. When a new employee joins and gets their company vehicle, you may need to give them a copy of the latest fleet policy, a list of vehicles to choose from, a fuel card, an expenses claim form, a business mileage form and so on. Not so many years ago you would have issued a thick fleet manual but today this can be held on your intranet so you need only direct the driver to the relevant intranet pages and get them to sign a note confirming they have read this information.

Once they have their new car you will need to keep in touch, sending reminders when a service or MoT is due or overdue and when the vehicle is due for replacement. Much of this is now done by email. By holding sent emails in your Sent Mail folder until the driver has responded as required, you will be certain that you have not missed anything.

Even when email is not appropriate, such as when a tax disc is to be sent to the driver, it is still useful to email the driver to confirm the tax disc has been sent and to ask for an email confirming receipt.

Most fleet software packages send emails directly to the driver and log the fact that these have been sent.

MOTOR INSURERS' BUREAU (MIB)

There has always been a problem with uninsured vehicles operating on Britain's roads. Whilst many of these cars are now being detected by police cars using automatic number plate recognition (ANPR) systems they still cause significant problems and expense for honest drivers when there is an accident.

It is estimated that the cost of uninsured vehicles in Britain exceeds £500m and this cost is borne by honest motorists paying higher insurance premiums – an average £30 per car. It is illegal for an uninsured car to be on the road and the MIB exists to combat this crime.

All vehicles must be registered on the Motor Insurance Database by law. See www.miic.org.uk for the registration procedure. The obligation to register your cars on the database is yours. Ask your insurer or broker whether they plan to do this for you.

You need to submit the required data, either to your broker or direct to the database, and whenever you change your vehicles you must update the database. If you fail to register a vehicle you will be liable to a fine.

Cars that are to be held by fleets for less than 14 days do not need to be registered.

COMPENSATION RECOVERY UNIT (CRU)

The CRU is a division of the Department of Work and Pensions. Road accidents cost the NHS hundreds of millions of pounds a year and the CRU makes enquiries after an accident to see who was responsible. If a company car driver was involved and their employer has comprehensive insurance, the CRU will claim the cost of NHS treatment from the insurer. If the employer self-insures the fleet, the CRU will claim from the employer.

So one of the unexpected side effects of self-insuring your company car fleet is that you could start receiving charges from the CRU. The maximum charge is around £35,000.

Appendix: Further Information

Association of Car Fleet Operators (ACFO)

Many fleet managers value having contact with other fleet managers. This was the guiding thought behind the establishment of the Association of Car Fleet Operators. Their regional structure offers the opportunity to network with other fleet managers locally. They hold frequent meetings with speakers who are experts in their fields.

www.acfo.org.

Institute of Car Fleet Management (ICFM)

An independent body that offers an education and training scheme for fleet managers. They provide courses at introductory, certificate and diploma level, targeted at three groups: newcomers to the industry, people with operational fleet responsibility and general managers responsible for fleets. www.icfmonline.co.uk

British Vehicle Rental and Leasing Association (BVRLA)

The trade association of the UK contract hire, rental and fleet management industry.

It represents its members on major policy issues, raises standards of operation and service and promotes and protects members' interests. www.bvrla.co.uk

Finance & Leasing Association (FLA)

The FLA is a trade association representing finance and leasing companies. www.fla.org.uk

The Institute of the Motor Industry (IMI)

The professional body for people employed in the automotive and associated industries. Offers education and training programmes covering technical, management, sales, customer service, administration and training and development. www.motor.org.uk.

The Motorists' Forum

An advisory non-departmental public body that provides independent advice to the Government on transport policy. Its members are drawn from a variety of organisations including motoring organisations, the petroleum industry, disabled drivers, the police, the Highways Agency and local government. It debates motoring issues with government. www.cfit.gov.uk/mf

Institute of Logistics and Transport

The Institute advises the government on transport policy and publishes a journal and a wide range of papers on transport and logistics. It runs training and development courses and has local branches throughout the country. www.iolt.org.uk.

Financial Services Authority (FSA)

The FSA regulates the financial services industry. Many lessors are owned by banks and are therefore regulated by the FSA. Should you believe that a financial institution is conducting business in a manner that may be illegal or damaging to the well-being of its customers or depositors, you may wish to contact the FSA to report your concerns. www.fsa.gov.uk.

Energy Savings Trust (EST)

The Energy Saving Trust was set up after the 1992 Earth Summit in Rio de Janeiro, to help reduce carbon dioxide emissions in the UK. It is of interest to fleets because it operates the TransportEnergy Powershift scheme. www.est.org.uk.

Vehicle & Operator Services Agency (VOSA)

This government agency promotes and enforces compliance with commercial operator licensing requirements, processes applications for lorry and bus licences, registers bus services, operates and administers all vehicle testing schemes, supervises the MoT Testing Scheme, enforces the law to ensure vehicles comply with legal standards and regulations, enforces drivers' hours and licensing requirements, provides training and advice for commercial operators, and investigates vehicle accidents, defects and recalls. www.vosa.gov.uk

The Occupational Road Safety Alliance (ORSA)

ORSA brings together employers, trade unions, local authorities, police forces, safety organisations and professional and trade associations to help employers manage at-work road risk. It facilitates networking between key stakeholders, encourages joint working to raise awareness of the need for action on work-related road safety and promotes the exchange of information on new initiatives and best practice. www.orsa.org.uk

Driver & Vehicle Licensing Agency (DVLA)

An Executive Agency of the Department for Transport (DfT), it facilitates road safety and law enforcement by maintaining registers of drivers and vehicles, and collects vehicle excise duty (car tax). www.dvla.gov.uk

HPI Database

You can check if the car you are buying has been stolen, written-off, clocked or has outstanding finance at www.hpicheck.com

British Independent Motor Traders Association (BIMTA)

Provides services for people buying imported vehicles (www.bimta.com)

UK Government Website

'Public services all in one place'. Includes driving licence Conviction and Endorsement codes. www.direct.gov.uk

Online Vehicle Relicensing

You can renew a tax disc online at www.vehiclelicence.gov.uk

Centre for Automotive Management; University of Buckingham Business School

Fleet industry surveys, research and publications. University validated awards can be offered for groups from individual organisations or on open programmes at certificate, diploma and degree level in the sector. Holds workshops, forums and short courses on topics of interest to fleet executives.

Contact: Professor Peter N C Cooke, KPMG Professor of Automotive Management; peter.cooke@buckingham.ac.uk

All makes fleet management approached from a new perspective... yours

Daimler Fleet Management (DFM) provides fleet funding for cars and light commercial vehicles from all leading manufacturers. Ranked Number 8 in the Fleet News FN50 listing of UK leasing companies by fleet size, DFM currently operates a UK fleet of over 49,000 vehicles; part of a pan-European fleet approaching 470,000 units.

Our fleet funding options and additional services include:

- Contract hire (for both personal and business users)
- Contract purchase
- Full outsourcing
- Fleet management
- Sale and leaseback

- Daily rental
- Fuel cards and management
- Accident management
- Vehicle maintenance
- Driver safety and duty of care assessments
- Employee affinity schemes

At a time when the regulatory and business challenges of operating company vehicles are increasing, DFM offers customers high levels of support in implementing financial, HR and operational strategies for their fleets and employee drivers. Fleets are frequently funded by a range of financial methods and may include a percentage of employees driving their own vehicles for business purposes. DFM develops cost-effective solutions to meet individual customer requirements, giving comprehensive management support, online resources and driver services to fleets of every configuration.

Whilst large enough to secure economies of scale for the benefit of customers, DFM provides genuinely personal service from a dedicated account manager, in-depth consultative advice, and transparent, measured service levels.

GETTING THE BEST FROM YOUR FLEET

Through consulting and analysis, DFM will help develop a strategy to ensure your fleet runs smoothly and cost effectively, evaluating the following areas:

FINANCE

- Whole life costs: examining the comparative whole life benefits of a range of models being considered for your fleet
- Fleet policy analysis: assessing the optimum policy strategies for current company requirements
- Funding methods: selecting the best finance options and investigating a range of funding formulae for a company fleet
- Budget & tax analysis: utilising opportunities provided by the current finance and tax environment
- Manufacturer discounts: negotiating favourable terms on acquiring and replacing vehicles

HUMAN RESOURCES

- Car policy strategies: structuring, banding and grading car policies for job entitlement and optimum HR benefits
- Employee motivation: promoting car policy incentives to motivate existing employees and encourage high calibre recruitment
- Driver support: offering support and information services to employee drivers
- Duty of care: advising on employer responsibilities for health and safety, including driving licence checks, enforcing vehicle roadworthiness, mobile phone use and remedial driver training
- Legislation: updates on regulations and issues affecting your fleet and drivers, such as the smoking ban in vehicles driven for business purposes

- Servicing, repair and maintenance: helping you to maintain your vehicles in optimum condition, ensuring their road worthiness and maximising residual value at contract end

- Route planning: advising on vehicle tracking and satellite navigation technologies

- Online systems: supplying reports, quotations, rental reservations and rapid service booking for drivers

- Environment policies: minimising CO_2 emissions, offering advice on hybrid and alternative fuel models and the development of green bandings in your car policy

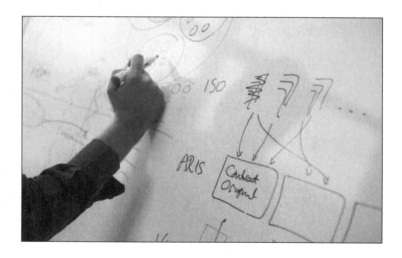

For more information call 0870 609 9911

email general.enquiries@daimler.com

or visit www.daimlerfleetmanagement.co.uk

Managing Your Company Cars

2nd edition published 2005. 520 pages. 172,000 words. £60.00

ISBN 1 902528 21 2

Published by Eyelevel Books in association with Daimler Fleet Management.

It available from www.amazon.co.uk, www.tourick.com and good bookshops.

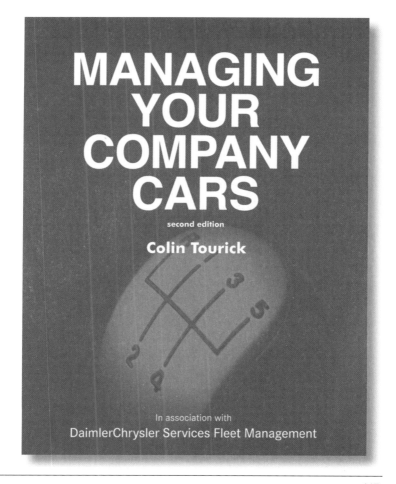

'Every profession should have a reference book; if you're in fleet management, this is it!'

James Langley, Chairman, Training & Education Committee,
Institute of Car Fleet Management

'This book is essential reading for all fleet decision-makers. It is the single most authoritative information source for all fleet funding and operational issues. Now fully updated, established fleet chiefs and those new to the job should have this latest edition at their fingertips.'

Ashley Martin, Industry analyst/consultant,
Former editor of Fleet News.

'If ever a book deserved a place on the book shelves of car lessors and lessees it is Managing Your Company Cars. The work is a tour de force of vehicle finance. A comprehensive guide for newcomers and the experienced alike.'

LeasingLife

'Managing Your Company Cars is the 'number one' reference book for the fleet industry, without question. It has an exhaustive range of information and is an invaluable addition to the bookcase of any fleet professional regardless of their role.'

Paul Ashton, Managing Director, Equalease Limited

Are you sure your fleet costs are under control?

There are many ways to reduce your costs without reducing the quality of the cars you offer your drivers.

Are you sure you are using the best method to fund your fleet vehicles?

No one method is right for each company. You may need to use different methods for different cars to minimise your costs.

Are you worried about your duty of care to your company car drivers?

You have to minimise the risks. You may need to carry out a comprehensive risk review.

We hope this book will help you solve your fleet problems.

But it can only provide general guidance.

There is no substitute for tailor made advice from an impartial, independent source.